LOVEPARENT

How To Be The Parent You Hope To Be

Written by
Betsy Otter Thompson

Edited by
Shirley W. Kuhn

The beauty of any idea is in knowing how to enjoy it.

ASCENSION PUBLISHING
Burbank, California

WARNING - RECLAIMER

LOVEPARENT is a book designed to help you find more serenity in your life. What you read herein is the author's concept of reality, and she takes responsibility for what happens in her life because of it. If you disagree, you aren't wrong. You just have a different perception of reality and your life will manifest your beliefs the same way. As you read LOVEPARENT, embrace what makes you feel wonderful because that's how you make the wonderful part of your life expand. What isn't helpful, isn't important. You know how to pick and choose for the benefit of your own experience and this is what the author hopes for you; a life filled with joy because you have honored what is meaningful.

LOVEPARENT
Ascension Publishing, Box 3001-890, Burbank, CA 91508

Copyright © 1991 by Betsy Otter Thompson

Publisher's Cataloging in Publication
    (Prepared by Quality Books Inc.)
Thompson, Betsy Otter, 1936-
Loveparent: How To Be The Parent You Hope To Be/written by Betsy Otter Thompson; Edited by Shirley W. Kuhn. --
p. cm
ISBN 1-879023-08-3 $8.95 Softcover   Includes Index

1. Child rearing. 2. Parenting. 3. Self Respect. I. Title

HQ769   649.1

                        90-82467
                        MARC

This book gives you the chance
to know two hearts;
the person who wrote it and
the person who committed her time
so that it came to you with such clarity.
Therefore, I dedicate "Loveparent" to
Shirley Kuhn
in the same way Shirley dedicated
herself to my project—in the spirit of two
who knew that whatever we created together
would grow as it found you,
and all that returned to us would have
your expanded hearts in it.

ACKNOWLEDGEMENTS

Dan Poynter, for his expertise to new publishers.

Jan Becker, for her willingness to contribute so many wonderful ideas.

Suzette Mahr, who found many ways to help this book.

Ara Norwood, for taking the time to help me when I wasn't sure how to proceed.

Robert Howard, whose art work is an inspiration for putting thoughts into form.

Willy Blumhoff, who brought his caring heart to my assistance.

Catharine and Ellis Marsalis, who helped me find my logo.

Cecille Bendavid, who understood my computer needs and cared for me before caring for a sale.

Pam Jones, who always responded to my plea for help, whether it was about computer capabilities or her own.

Hwei-Chu Meng and Jean Wells, for feed back that helped this book to grow.

CONTENTS

PREFACE

Nothing you learn from parenting can make your life work if it isn't already working. Nothing your children give you will feel valuable unless you believe in the valuable being you are. Nothing comes from them that you aren't able to give from yourself, and nothing except your own inner peace will give you a peaceful life with them.

I believe parenting is wonderful. It has enriched my life beyond words, but only because I've learned to accept each one of my children on their own terms. As I remembered they were here to satisfy their own inner longings and not to please me, we got along fine. And the only way I learned to release them was to do it for myself.

Although I tripped and stumbled with how I raised them, I never lost sight of the fact that they were totally individualized in how they looked, felt, thought and acted. And as I tried to respond to their needs, nothing ever worked the same for all of them except to love and accept whoever they were.

Being a parent is the only qualification I have for writing this book. I went through the process myself. And when I'm asked what gives me the right to present these ideas, my answer is the same. I've gone through the process of testing the theories and found that they worked.

When it comes to explaining how I found them, I can only say it happens the same way anyone finds his talent. He notices a little spark and has enough self-love to expand it. Some offer you their music, some their poetry, some their paintings, some their business skills, some their clerical, and on and on. This is my offering.

As you go about your life, every once in a while you're going to remember something you read in this book and wonder if what was shared could possible be true. And as you ponder what would happen if you believed it, your life will unfold to show you. Then every time you move into a more loving space from tenderly caring for your energy, I reap the rewards of your expansion by feeling a more loving universe in which to live.

Thank you.

Do You Want Children?

**THE ONLY "RIGHT" DECISION
IS THE ONE THAT LOVES YOU.**

***

The caring knowledge that comes with parenting knows many outlets, not just child rearing. To understand if this particular direction will love you, ask what you're going to gain from choosing it.

Are you interested in a commitment that will last for many years? Do you foresee happiness from nourishing the growth of another? Can you picture yourself in the role of a parent and find contentment from doing so? Do you think sharing your life will enhance what it already is? Do you anticipate activities you can enjoy together? Are you ready to welcome whatever gender arrives? Can you envision your tolerance level adjusting to the distraction a little one brings into your schedule? Is your mind flexible enough to enter into a loving relationship with a child who may be very different from you? Are you willing to encourage this progeny to become whatever his dream embraces? Have you prepared your life in such a way that having one will be a pleasure?

Or, do you want this because others are telling you it's important? Have relatives tried to convince you it's the only path that's fair to them? Are you worried you're getting older and missing what life is all about? Have you decided growing old alone is definitely unpleasant? Has someone convinced you that child rearing is the highlight of life? Do you think you'll fit in better with your relations with an expanded family? Who are you trying to please with your decision?

As you read over these questions, go back to where you hesitated and be honest with yourself. To deal with a possible reluctance now is to make sure you sustain yourself before taking on the responsibility of nurturing another. For procreation to become the joy it's meant to be, you must love the present beneficial expansion and this doesn't always include children.

If you've read this far and know that raising a family is the most important dream you have, it won't matter what you read, feel or hear from another. Commitment felt this strongly understands what it needs and acts accordingly.

If you're wavering back and forth, lacking the understanding of what it means to be a parent, answers are here to help you discover the direction that will tenderly caress you.

If you already have children, ideas in this book can make your shared experience all the more brilliant.

If nurturing others is definitely not your cup of tea, then perhaps you're reading this to improve your own self-parenting.

All fairness to yourself is what creates an equitable

life, whether it's about child rearing, getting married, changing jobs, moving on, or just having a pleasant day.

What can parenting give you that can't be found any other way? Nothing. It isn't for everyone, and it isn't valuable unless you find satisfaction through it. It cares for those who take it by teaching the reflection concept; whatever you know to be true for yourself is what you cherish in others.

This familial role isn't imperative for a perfectly delightful life. It's just one in millions that Earth offers now. If you'd rather work with other adventures, love yourself enough to pursue them. There are many ways to embrace the same beauty that comes from family life, and you'll find the ones that bless you if you stay honest about your instincts.

Parenting embraces the concept of nourishing. Therefore, any idea that supports and sustains you while here, is this. When the time comes to choose the path that suits you, make sure to consider what brings you happy expectation. That's what makes the parenting idea work, whichever one you choose.

Why is it important to be a parent? It isn't. Not any more than it is to be whatever makes life beautiful. It's just an option, that's all. And you'll react to it the same as you react to any other. If it gets you all excited and happy, it's definitely for you. If you take it because you're trying to please another, you may have a hard time enjoying it when it arrives. But then this is true for any theory you

3

appropriate when the reason for taking it is uncaring. You aren't here to please anyone but yourself.

What can you do if one person wants a child and the other one doesn't? You bring your truth to one another so God has a chance to enter these discussions. Have compassion for the needs of the other and recognize that just because you want one thing, doesn't mean everyone in your life must too. The way to work through this is the same process of working through any discrepancy in shared beliefs. You talk so that each understands what the partner needs to fulfill himself. And if the paths are too far apart to lovingly coexist, you release the other to pursue his own tender dream as you carry on with your own.

All exercises here on Earth are about the same thing; honoring the self so that the whole knows whereof it originates. Isn't humanness just the joining of millions of entities trying to live together in harmony? And if this is so, isn't it just about finding a peaceful co-existence? And if this is so, isn't it about the search for the goodness within? And if we're all searching for the worthiness of ourselves, aren't we all trying to connect up to the beauty we call love? And isn't God the personification of love?

As you read what follows, consider that you are this beautiful energy trying to find the essence of yourself. And if you are, then so is everyone. And what better place to start for appreciating this fact than with the infant who still remembers his all adoring aura.

When you ask if you should reproduce, examine your motives. Is it duty, achievement, guilt or self-love inspiring your goals? To gain a fuller understanding of which, perhaps the following questions can help.

What happens when I become a parent? You offer a nurturing womb of love for spirit to rediscover its Godhood in humanness.

Why would I want to do this? Because it's fun to watch the creator expand, and as you join the process you get to expand right alongside the ones you love the most.

What can I gain from being a parent? Whatever you're willing to give it, because the child will return your blessings a thousand fold.

How do I know if I'll be a good one? If you sense the desire, that's enough. Everything else will arrive when the yearning is felt.

How can I be sure that everything needed will arrive? You can only test this theory and see what happens when you trust it. That's how you find everything and parenting isn't any different.

What are the benefits from having children? They come in every category you believe in and God doesn't tell you how they must unfold. Some are looking for blessings that others aren't, so each grouping has their own blissful thoughts to gain from the union.

What commitment is necessary? The one that says you rejoice to offer your body, love and guidance to another beautiful soul who is trying to remember the eternal absolute personified in humanness.

What understanding do I need to achieve this? The awareness that says you're ready, willing and excited to begin. God doesn't need reasons for growth, he just needs his desire to participate.

What will I learn from being a parent? You will learn whatever you believe is important to learn, and only you can grasp the meaning of what that is. Each soul knows what it craves to gain from whatever game it participates in. Look for your reward in your excitement about life.

As God watches the beauty you find from parenting others, he knows how to bring you the parenting you need, and this is the beauty called forever. As you open to all that your children bring you, all that is God, is yours.

CHILDREN BRING BEAUTY
TO THOSE WHO WELCOME THIS VEHICLE.

CHAPTER 1

Conception

**EXPANSION BEGAN
THE MOMENT GOD SAID "INTROSPECT."**

***

Conception is the seed of a thought. It happens when spirit has any thought for expansion. Its purpose is to give energy the chance to learn more about its own true nature, so wherever it's happening it's a rebirth into exploration. One of the places it happens is on Planet Earth.

This book is focusing on the human condition and all that this particular opportunity offers in terms of parenting. But God's answer to growth is what conception is all about, so kindness to yourself doesn't stop at the world as you know it. If energy is ready for genesis in a different arena, it has millions of options to choose from. It just takes its progress into whatever milieux sounds interesting and the process begins. God's love for himself is insatiable, so whatever beginning he loves, he finds.

Rebirthing in this particular dream begins the moment light says, I have a longing to know myself in matter with the same understanding I enjoy without it. And I also long to expand it on Earth. With this determination firmly planted within, spirit begins to investigate what would be instructive to find, when arriving. This dream encompasses decisions for family, friends, characteristics, gender, country, race and nationality that will inspire that heart towards more love for the energy it calls its own.

Every human with you is this force expanding and each has their own perception of loving progress. Therefore, all are planning according to the knowledge they're looking for which is why the experience manifests so individually.

The growth for the parent comes from seeing God in his complete identity as the all adoring energy that emerges.

To believe that the gift of life sources through the coupling Gods is to be in a trance. This energy has chosen what will stimulate the discovery of its own inner beauty. He wants the affirmation he knew all too well before coming; that he is the mastermind of his own existence whatever form he has taken, and wherever he has arrived. The autonomous caring you're able to give this baby takes him into the sovereign realm he just left. And if you encourage his independence he will help you remember your own.

While the child has his own reasons for coming, the parents have wonderful benefits too. First, they have the excitement from knowing they're helping one of their very own find human beauty. Secondly, they go through the miraculous process of helping this entity grow through their nourishment. Thirdly, they have the fun of spending time with this adorable energy after it arrives. And finally, they let themselves in for a continual family of fellowship as they grow with and learn from their children.

That's why so many welcome this bursting forth of sensational vibrations. As they receive these young Gods in a joint effort towards remembered autonomy, opportunities present themselves for further expansion. Each is just as miraculous as the conception that brought them together. God is just finding more ways to appreciate new potentials, as he finds love and acceptance from this one.

What this lovely journey through the womb brings, is wrapped up in choices; how he wants to look when he gets here and what he wants to influence him after he arrives.

The physical characteristics are chosen through genes. The emotional choices come through the heart of God. Earth is one part of the totality known as everything. And in this everything, spirit can pick and choose his strengths and weaknesses. Why would he choose weaknesses? Because he wants to overcome what he doesn't have in illusion, to find what he does have in reality. He doesn't expect to find a perfect person when he comes. Nor does he want to expect to find perfection in others. He hopes to remember that whatever he did choose is helping him and whatever he didn't, he doesn't need.

Helping him do what? Helping him enjoy his fantasy. Helping him enjoy his energy. Helping him enjoy yours. While he's planning this trip, he can't imagine not having a good time when he gets here. Why? Because he believes so strongly in the beauty of himself.

How could he not? Everyone he knows has been encouraging him to remember his Godhood. Everyone he knows looks exactly like him. Everyone he knows is trying to grow also. Everyone he knows is birthing into whatever sounds delightful. Everyone he knows has the aura of God in his totality. The womb represents his birth into a dream for remembering all of this. Why does he want to come here to remember? For the same reason you like to bring love into whatever you undertake.

What is happening with spirit while all this matter growth is taking place in his dream inside the womb? What would you imagine energy doing as it waited for something so heavenly as this? What do you do as you wait for wonderful eventualities? Can happiness be in waiting for love, or is it in living it every moment?

Spirit is never static even when he's planning the miracle of birth, so while he may love visiting the uterus now and then, he is still taking his energy into whatever exploration sounds intriguing. You wouldn't want to keep this resplendence holed up in a small little space without anything to do except sit there and wait for his body to develop, would you? That would be like saying you couldn't have the fun of every moment you live, regardless of whether it was momentous or not.

Until the instant of birth, this ecstatic being is fulfilling himself in whatever delightful activity catches his fancy. When the child comes forth into freedom at birth, the free spirit enters his own newly formed body and begins his unique independent journey in the thought he first conceived of when he felt the longing to return.

Can you imagine the drama there is for this adorable being as he watches the mother get ready to deliver his own idea? Quite the same feeling you get when you're in the middle of watching something you've worked on burst forth into completeness. It's pretty dazzling, not only for the purposeful God who's joining this baby, but for all those coming soon after and all those who enjoyed the thought processes that got him there.

Who can have the kindness he deserves unless he understands where to find it? This is what energy that's about to become matter has on his mind. Will I remember all that I know now? Will I look to myself for what will love me? Will I take responsibility for my reflection? How soon will I believe the lie that I'm not God? How willing will I be to reconsider? Will I trust my instincts with my built-in salvation? How closely will I listen to the optimistic side of my nature? Will I trust that whatever arrives in my life is welcome? Will I forget the principle behind a balanced universe where everything I express, I receive? This is the reinforcing spirit undergoes as the last growth takes place inside the womb. This is re-birthing at its most loving; light in constant communication with the love he knows as completeness.

Beauty exists in whatever state it has chosen, so as the soul goes about doing last minute love sessions, he's still growing in expanded thought. While waiting to join the dream, he enjoys the anticipation of joining beloved friends. And because he wants to bond with them immediately upon arrival, savoring their Godliness is the wisdom of now. When they first meet in matter, the brilliance they share is glorious to behold; billions of iridescent sparkles of love emitting from both their auras as God reunites with himself.

THE ATOM IS THE FIRST IDEA GOD HAD.

FROM THEN ON

IT WAS JUST MORE OF THE SAME.

SO TO MAKE MORE OF YOURSELF,

IS TO ADORE THE ORIGINAL CREATION.

CHAPTER 2

The New Idea

***

All that you ever wanted to know you can find by looking into the eyes of a newborn baby. What you'll see is God staring back at you. God as he truly knows himself to be; all knowing, autonomous, powerful, adoring, compassionate, eager to grow, eager to share, and eager to love. What this infant knows is what you're trying to remember, and if you can listen to his heart instead of forcing him to listen to yours, you will again find yourself.

This energy has just come from a state of completeness the likes of which you're searching for. To find it is to understand what creates it, and this little bundle of joy can show you exactly what does the trick. The secret to understanding his contentment comes from taking the behavior of this child and making it your own. When he looks at you with happy expectancy, show him you only expect to love him with the same happy feelings. When he looks to you for guidance, give him back the innocent and pure trust he's giving to you. When he looks for information about the world he's entered, show him what your heart believes is beautiful.

It may seem that this kind of thought isn't communicated at birth, but words aren't needed to convey love. His heart is knowingly connected to the beauty of himself and, therefore, interacts with the harmony in you. He reads your aura and understands your every thought.

He arrives believing he'll find the same precious energy he is. Are you assuring him this is so? He arrives believing your heart has welcomed him with delightful expectancy. Are you confirming this belief? He arrives with total knowledge of how beautiful his energy is. Are you agreeing with him? He arrives thinking that everything about him is a thought that's wonderful to behold. Are you delighting in his choices? He arrives believing that you want him to increase the joy in your life. Are you welcoming how he'll do this? He arrives believing he can do anything he sets out to do. Are you confirming that his energy can be all that he dreams of finding? He believes everything about you is wonderful too. Are you proving him correct?

If you wonder if you're all these things he believes you are, look into his eyes again. See if you can't take for yourself the respect and admiration he shows towards you. He has just seen the "you" that is the energy like his, so he knows whereof he feels.

Let yourself bask in the emotion this brings. Remind yourself he must know what he's sensing since he's just left the world where knowledge is complete. And if you can help him respect his own memory of how things truly are, you jog your own remembrance of the world as God views it.

What does this knowingness really see as he gazes at you with those trusting eyes? When you first enter humanness your eyesight is divine, so what you see has the focus of what God sees. And if this is so, the knowledge it gives is more profound than what Earthly focusing alone considers informative. This baby sees the only "you" that really matters; the "you" that is your thoughts.

Imagine how delightful it would be to read all the auras around you; to understand the feelings of everyone. This is the eyesight of your infant, and even after his focusing apparatus gets used to his new environment, he continues to read auras for quite a while. The longer he loves what he reads there, the longer he keeps this skill.

There are some who never lose this ability, there are some who intermittently gain it back, and there are some who lose it almost immediately to begin communicating more comfortably.

Encourage your child to keep this eyesight by feeding him thoughts that reinforce it. This is God's way of corresponding, and it's the most powerful tool he'll ever have for creating the blissful life he hopes to enjoy. If you bring him the inspiring voice of devotion from the moment he enters your life, he will return your devoted loyalty a thousand fold.

As he looks up to you with those curious adoring

eyes, he sees the beauty of your totality. It reassures him that nothing different is happening here from the beauty he just left because for a while it looks the same to him. Everywhere he looks he sees halos of luminescent color and sparkling silver light beams swirling and dancing around his own. His little cosmos soaks it up with eager enthusiasm just like he did before birth. He hopes to continue doing this for his entire journey and his heart believes it's entirely possible. He still remembers God's promise that whatever he gave out into his personal universe would create the personal universe that surrounded him.

This precious being can't feel anything but ecstasy. The first sounds may seem like crying to you, but he's just testing his vocal cords for the fun of it. After all, he's been looking forward to this for over nine months and it's a glorious cry of successful establishment. Don't you enjoy shouting your pleasure at times, screaming to the world how magnificent life is?

This moment of entering matter is the exultant triumph of spirit in a new and exciting thought. He feels the glory of it very powerfully those first few moments. He's just taken all his hopes and dreams into the body he created to manifest them, and to him his idea looks like heaven on Earth.

How do you feel when your imagination has successfully actualized an adventure? Aren't you beside yourself with joy? Aren't you excited to use it?

Aren't you looking forward to sharing it? Aren't you bursting with enthusiasm about what your success will bring more of? This is the intoxicating joy this baby experiences, and whatever of this you can bring into your own aura will replenish your excitement about matter too.

Try to listen to how this energy expresses itself when first born. When he's sleepy, he doesn't let anything disturb his rest. When he's awake, he's eager to understand his surroundings. When he's hungry, he cries until fed. When he's happy, he gurgles with contentment. When he's angry, he verbalizes it. So despite the fact that words aren't shared, you get a good sense of how he feels.

Never does he think, how terrible, that doesn't sound like a nice way to act. He just responds to whatever is going on inside his emotions and, therefore, moves from one to another with ease. Don't you think this sounds like a wonderful way to live? This child is showing you how it's done, and it happens because instant response is his method for living.

Anger is displaced in seconds as he experiences whatever feeling comes up. One minute crying, the next a happy smile. This is freedom in its truest sense, exploding power going in whatever direction keeps itself in comfort and ease.

Take some lessons from your newborn and watch how he lets love run his life. Self-caring isn't just respect and honor for your being, it's allowing your being to exist any way you feel at ease within yourself. Who can have all that life offers unless he lets himself experience all that life is?

What this first stage of new birth can bring is a glimpse of how God believes in free expression. Every healthy outlet you allow, increases your ability to be who you really are. Why? Because the more exercise you give autonomous action, the stronger it is at performing its task.

Your emotions want to feel liberated to go in whatever direction they sense more joy, and the more you practice what helps this happen, the better you get at doing it. Watch how this bundle of energy makes himself comfortable and you have the clue for doing the same for yourself.

NOTHING QUITE BEATS
THE EMERGENCE OF SPIRIT INTO MATTER.
IT'S THE DREAM REFLECTED IN FORM.

CHAPTER 3

Genes

***

This miraculous birthing image is the catharsis of God in knowingness. The process originates through character choices and genes. Therefore, all that you are is your tool for learning. And since this beautifully assembled genetic structure is really just a collection of ideas transposed into form, it can change if spirit takes a new approach to his human journey.

You may think it's impossible for genes to alter themselves, but God's power hasn't left you simply because you've gone into matter. The process of editing is as easy as finding what loves you more. That's what got the original set together, and that's what gets you more of what will love you.

Whenever they modify, you can be sure experiments in thought are occurring as God looks into better ways of finding his goals. Genes are optional patterns, and they aren't written in stone or permanently programmed for your entire life. You can rearrange and revise whenever your all powerful God decides to.

Try to imagine the matter you represent as a

reflection of whatever thoughts your energy is happy dealing with. You may have one desired look when you begin your journey only to find that some altering here and there will accelerate your progress. This modifying interprets differently from person to person, but when bodily any changes manifest, energy is acting autonomously to the betterment of its own understanding. Their purpose can be found when you're willing to evaluate their presence. What would you ask if you knew God was waiting to answer you?

What do these changes look like? They vary according to what you believe is loving progress, so anything from hair texture to physical health can be a gene altering.

How can health changes be determined by genes? If genes are just patterns you decide to change or dismiss, you can make them whatever you think is wonderful whenever you're ready to find more of whatever this means.

The purpose of your genetic structure is to highlight your trip into matter by bringing all the accoutrements that enhance your journey. If your God within finds a new embellishment, nothing can stop the flow of inventiveness, and certainly not something as adaptable as genes.

What is your contribution towards what your child has chosen? Very little, except as the storehouse from which to select. But your storehouse is the one that delighted him, so it's the miracle he was looking for. Revel in the thought that all he wanted to find looked easy through you.

How did he do this? The same way you gather ideas together you want to live with. You embrace the ones you love and make them a part of your consciousness. This is what your child has done to create the form he knew would educate his soul. Because belief in himself is so knowing and trust in his aura so powerful, he's counting on these gifts to propel him into whatever will nourish his edification.

When did he do this? When he felt your willingness to subsidize his early years. It didn't take long to collect the genes he wanted because great care and decisiveness got him to the point of entering the human fantasy. The wisdom behind every decision was that which understands eternity.

Where do you fit in with what he's brought with him? This answer will show itself with the exact ease with which you delight in whatever he brought. If you look for his recognition of valuable assets instead of preconceived attributes you wanted him to have, the contribution you make is enormous.

As the parent, you have the opportunity to help him discover his choices and delight in them. If you don't, he may do it on his own. How quickly, depends on his remembered love for his own enlightenment and tenacity to honor self.

Genes are no more fixed than your desire to take a vacation and follow through. Whether or not this is the present mass perception, the fact remains that the force of a belief is all it takes to bring it about.

The young child who hasn't yet heard he can't change and grow, is a miracle of finesse before your very eyes. He is showing you the explosiveness of God in completeness as he changes eye color, hair color, shape, size and insight. You just accept this expansion as a part of maturing, so no one is surprised to see it happen. If the mass consciousness accepted that gene changes were common for anyone, it would be just as happily expected.

Bring your open mind to the many possibilities your child has regarding his mixing and rearranging of genes, and then watch how excitedly he goes about proving you right.

FOR EVERY GENE YOU CHOOSE,

A THOUGHT IS BROUGHT TO FORM.

The First Communication

HARMONY IS A MENTAL CONDITION
BROUGHT BY THOUGHTS, NOT WORDS.

***

Put yourself in the place of this little baby who has just joined you. There he is, eating, sleeping, growing, learning, starting to make sounds to explain his thoughts, and curious about every single nuance that enters his aura. Before honing in on what opinions he's going to have about his body, his talent, his intelligence, and his health, he's noticing yours. If they agree with his, he's going to be a very contented baby. If not, he's going to begin doubting himself rather early on. His way of expressing his doubt is to challenge you with his opinions. A baby challenges you by giving you his most precious side immediately.

How does he do this? Well, what do you think is precious about him? His trust in you? His belief in you? His unconditional love for you?

In cooperation with his lively mind that is reassuring him he's still God, he trusts you completely and believes you are too. And whether or not you agree, he still loves you with total devotion. He returns your affections despite your irritations, angers, and frustrations and comes to your assistance with love and adoration over and over, showing you what he believes is your shared experience.

Watch your child carefully, and see if he doesn't communicate: I adore you whatever you do, think or feel. I express myself whatever is happening. I have my needs, however much you have yours, and believe we can satisfy ourselves together. I don't care what anyone looks like; if their heart is kind I love them. I treasure your closeness and feel comfortable to nestle in your relaxed emotions. If you need to explode I don't care; I have the same need and know how good it makes me feel. All I have is yours to share. All I know is yours to enjoy. And all I am is yours to love.

This is how God dotes on you and your child is showing you what his beauty looks like. This baby's first communication is: Here is the peace you admire so. Here is the confidence you're searching for. Here is the simplicity you long for. Here it is; in the ideas I have about myself. I see the love in everyone. I welcome whoever wants to share a laugh. I'll offer the beauty I find with whomever comes along. Let me help you with whatever troubles you. Let me give you tenderness for your hurts and pains. Let me hug you when you're disappointed. Let me reassure you I love you no matter what.

This child has feelings of unconditional devotion for quite a while. They'll stay for however long his determination lasts. Some keep it for a lifetime, even though many events come along to shake this confidence. Some lose it completely to take on worldly thoughts about hate, prejudice, injustice, and destruction. Some go back and forth with varying degrees of contentment, depending on their inner resolve to remember the emotions that made life wonderful. But the gift to you as the parent is the first hand look at how God behaves when he still remembers his identity. If you can give your love the same way, your life will become more like his.

God wants you to have the same enrichment, the same freedom, the same serenity, and the same insight. Take your little ones seriously. Don't brush off their behavior as the innocence of youth. They're here for the same reason you are; to find the core of their being. They have the answer when they first come because nothing has destroyed their belief in themselves.

You are the one who needs a refresher course about the joy in life. You are the one who needs to reconsider the meaning of honor and integrity. You are the one who needs to learn how to communicate. You are the one who needs to understand the true meaning of discipline. You are the one who needs an education about the history of the universe.

These children know it until you convince them they're too young to grasp what they're talking about. Listen to them, my wonderful adventuresome parents. They're coming with the information of God in complete knowingness.

What will your baby learn about himself from you? Will he see your belief in his miraculous form? Will you show him you're thrilled with whatever gender he selected? Will you reassure him that his body is heavenly, whatever eyes, nose, mouth, size and color?

Are you ready to encourage whatever talent emerges? Have you released your expectations so he can have his own? Are you ready to delight in whatever he shows you is important to his growth?

How much is his intelligence wrapped up in your own ego and what others will think of you because of it? Have you already made plans for his higher education, or are you willing to wait and see if this is his ambition? Do you believe his common sense is what will make him successful at living, or have you convinced yourself intellect is the only aphrodisiac?

And most importantly, what are you communicating about health? Do you constantly worry and fret over him, conveying the message that something must be wrong? Or have you assured yourself that his health is the exact strength and vitality he wanted. Are your thoughts filled with the possibility of disease harming your beloved baby, or do you stay focused on the healthy strong infant he seems to be?

This progeny arrives knowing that everything he finds is a possibility he'll either select or discard. If he sees a parent who is fixated on disease, either the chance of it or the panic of it coming, he's more likely to adopt the same prospect. Why wouldn't he? He thinks you're God with wonderful games to play in. If your thoughts have the message worry, worry, worry about colds, it's fairly certain this infant will think it's a curiosity worth investigating.

He reads your aura and, therefore, knows what you focus on. He reacts to it for his own wisdom. Are you embracing the potentials you hope he'll take? It doesn't work by focusing on don't get sick, don't get sick. All he feels from this is tension. Remind yourself that illness is a supposition. If you don't carry that particular one around, at least he won't be finding it from you.

This caring energy came to you in perfect health in terms of loving choices. Are you agreeing or doubting his wisdom? If he chose some physical abnormality, this may look like a mistake of nature to you, but God is too wise to select without complete understanding of his needs.

Your first step towards contentment is to accept that his soul is knowing for himself. If it's correctable, you'll all gain in love as entities join to assist you. If it isn't, trust that your child has reasons. If you don't, you encourage him to feel like a victim. And this cultivates resentment, loss of self-respect and feelings that life is unfair.

When you can see through the outward inconvenience to the strength and insight his soul is finding, he takes the attitude that everything is a wonderful challenge and finds the growth he was looking for.

All of this is happening in the first stages of development, and while this child may not be reasoning his thoughts out in the same manner you do, he's still watching you for what looks intriguing.

If you want to understand the knowing way his mind works, feel what your intellect does when perfect contentment is your expression. As you lie in a hammock in the afternoon sun and enjoy the fullness of the experience, where are your thoughts? As you sit on the beach and watch the sunset with clouds in multitudes of colors and shapes, how does your heart feel? When you wake on a day that has special meaning, what is your mood of expectancy?

This is the contemplation of your newborn; joy, love and excitement as he starts to get used to his new surroundings. He doesn't think in terms of choices yet. He's still completely entranced in his emotions and they tell him everything he needs to know.

All the auras surrounding him look the same. He still has the focus of God where everyone is his mother, father, sister and brother. He has just come from the plane of understanding where everyone who lives is his friend and equal. He won't differentiate until someone tells him that others are separate and dissimilar and he believes the lie. Your opportunity is to assure him that nothing extra has been added to his birthing philosophy, and all that he sees is the love of God.

YOUR CHILD COMMUNICATES
WITH THE LOVE YOU REPRESENT.
WHEN YOU SPEAK BACK,
LET HIM SEE YOUR AGREEMENT

CHAPTER 5

Forming Ideas

**IDEAS ARE ALIVE
SO GIVE THEM THE FOOD THEY CRAVE.**

***

Coming into conscious awareness of what to expect while here is a gradual process, and one that can change from minute to minute even when you're well into middle age. But this is especially true for a youngster as he starts looking around at what this adventure includes.

Each God who takes this reproduction route believes his parents are the ones who can start him off with the wisest challenges. He wants exposure to your thoughts as he first comprehends his surroundings, so your beliefs give him his first glimpse of what life in matter is all about.

Suppose you were going to a party, got all dressed up in your best clothes, took time to create a nice appearance, and joyously transported yourself to where it was happening. However, when you walked into the festivities, what you found was a room full of complaining, unhappy, and disgruntled people. Even though you knew your energy was wonderful, you'd still feel that somehow you arrived at the wrong party, wouldn't you?

And how about if you walked into a room full of

happy, joyous welcoming guests, celebrating your arrival? Well, this is what your baby does. He walks into the room of humanness in a wonderful mood, glad to be alive, thrilled to be expanding, and ecstatic about joining you. Which kind of a room is he finding when he gets here?

The first impression is a strong one although he's free to change his mind about whether he wants to stay in that room for very long. But for a while, he's agreed that's it's an interesting beginning. If he decides another setting has more inspiration, he'll start attracting other options. The "when" is very flexible, depending on how soon his energy knows that something else will love him more. Your need is to ask what kind of reception he's getting for the short time he trusts his learning with you.

As he looks around, what is he discovering about the party he's come to? This is how he forms his first conclusions. He knows how wonderful his energy is, that's true, but he's just beginning to formulate how he feels about what he's joined. Is he receiving messages that nobody is to be trusted, misery is everywhere, living is a drag, people are worthless, the world is warmongering, his neighbors are bigoted, his country is unfair, his life will be a struggle, and you're not sure you want him?

Or is he finding a warm, loving reception, filled with thoughts that say everyone is God, love is everywhere, living is exciting, people are delightful, the world is full of growth, the neighbors can't wait to meet him, his country has much to offer him, his life will give him wisdom, and you're thrilled he wanted to learn these ideas from you first?

How do you want your child to think? He will formulate his own concepts regardless of yours, but if you want to encourage independent thought for him, take some for yourself. Be an example of free thinking energy that knows what makes it happy and honors it. This is the hope he has for creating a rewarding encounter; the courage to stick to his own convictions about what's important.

When you formulate opinions, what makes you keep some and discard others? Don't you experiment, seeing what happens? This is what your newly growing child is doing every moment; testing to see what transpires when he believes this, and then that, and then this, and so on and so on and so on. And each time he tests a belief that adds to his pleasure, he keeps it. When something makes him miserable he drops it. What he wants from you is the same behavior on a consistent basis. This is his reassurance that testing is wise and loving.

When this child has some growing to do, he wants your support of his efforts. He thinks to be bigger is to be like you. If he's thrilled with how you are he'll look forward to it. If he sees you in discomfort, he'll wonder if this is his fortune too and be more cautious of trusting your direction.

Being gifted as a parent is the same thing as being kind to yourself because this is the ultimate reward.

He wants to remember that his energy is God's, and if you help him remember this, he'll treat you like the God you are.

Remaining his friend is about understanding friendship. What do you value in relationships? Your child becomes an adult very quickly and if you haven't established what makes for loving interchange, why would he think of you as someone with whom to cultivate his progress?

Everyone wants support from those they call friends. They want encouragement to try whatever sounds engaging, understanding when concepts don't work, and reassurance that anything is doable in the presence of determination. If you can't find it in your heart to support his trip this way, why would he think your friendship was valuable?

Question how you connect your children's goals in life with your own. How true have you been to yours? If you've honored what was important, you won't have difficulty doing it for them. But if you think you missed all your own best opportunities, you'll think that your offspring are doing the same.

To find serenity as a parent, it's important to understand that humanness is about individuality. Therefore, when you push your children to be like you or someone else, they're going to rebel. Everyone is here to be themselves and to discover just what that means. If you encourage this kind of growth, you'll never have to worry about their friendship.

If you have preconceived ideas about how your

children should live and make it impossible for them to affectionately disagree, you can count on distancing. The seeds for mistrust begin early in life, and whether or not you say how you feel, your child receives the message. If he senses he's fighting an impossible battle, you'll find yourself with a withdrawn and disturbed youngster. And the way to reach someone who believes he can't live up to another's expectations is to change your expectations. Start looking for what he does have to contribute, not what you think he should have. Start praising the talents he does have, and he'll start blossoming into the entity he's here to be.

You belabor your own path when you're obstinate about another's. Why? Because your aura always has the thought that something is going wrong. And when you hold onto the belief that things aren't turning out the way they should with others, the same belief consumes your own life.

Some believe parenting gives the right to certain expectations. After all, you brought them up, clothed and fed them. If you didn't show them what it means to be God, you didn't give them anything. That's all they're looking for.

If someone offered you a trip around the world but you needed a good meal, what good is their ticket? When much has been done to teach your children the value of their own independence, you've found the only true gift that's important. It's about showing them how to honor their own creative energy. This is their reason for being here. This is what all their choices are about.

Being happy on this Earth isn't as complicated as you think. It isn't about what you've accomplished in terms of career, money, and prestige. It's about the integrity you've managed to give yourself and this doesn't have any outward look to it. Whatever field of endeavor your children choose for creative expansion is the milieu they think would be fun to learn in. Regardless of which ones are chosen, the same learning is happening.

It's impossible to find self-love unless energy has freedom to expand into what feels comfortable, because that's where integrity lies. It's about self-discovery, not about emulating you. Children copy how you deal with your life and how you feel about others, but they can't create talents they don't have or personality traits they didn't include. What they hope to mimic is the ability to appreciate what they have, not the perception that they must be like you to be acceptable.

When the youngster senses approval for the package he created, your role has been successful. This is what leads your child into independence which is the goal of every being who ever lived.

COMING INTO HUMANNESS
IS CONSTRUCTIVE ACTIVITY.
ANYTHING ELSE THAT MAKES IT PLEASURABLE
IS THE SAME LOVE.

CHAPTER 6

Eating Habits

BRING YOUR TOLERANT COMPASSION
TO EATING.

IT BEGINS THE IDEA OF
SELF-NOURISHMENT

***

What is it that bothers you so much about the way others eat? The answer is the same regardless of whether you're talking about children, friends or total strangers; either they're eating the wrong food or they're eating it the wrong way. With young children, this translates into not eating what you think they should, or eating in a way that upsets you.

The infant, who first finds nourishment wrapped securely in his mother's arms, learns to associate food with comfort, warmth and closeness. Having decided that good things are connected to maternal proximity, he's eager to find more through this vehicle. To assure him that caring and affection will continue after weaning, begin the new routine with the same serenity. Let the child guide you as to when he's ready for more.

When the baby has enough milk you can't force him to drink more, can you? He just turns his head away or falls asleep and that's that. When you supplement his diet, he'll know when solid food gives him nourishment and he'll know how much is needed here too. Mutual trust begins this early, and honoring his intuition is just as important now as at any other time in his life. He's still operating on the instincts of God loving himself. You needn't worry if he's receiving the necessary vitamins and minerals. The foods he welcomes are the ones he needs.

If your child believes you understand when he's hungry and when he isn't, dietary peace reigns. To continue in the same cooperation, maintain the same principles. Introduce whatever you want, but allow him the privilege of deciding if it pleases him. His taste senses are his own and he isn't confused about what he prefers. If you ignore his independence in this basic function, mistrust will damper his enthusiasm for your guidance.

When it comes to introducing sweets and you worry he'll only choose what's bad for him, keep in mind that for quite a while you're in control of the menu. What he hasn't tasted, he won't care about. What he doesn't see, he can't choose. Even if it's presented on a constant basis for one reason or another, eventually he opts for the healthy alternative.

There is a multitude of dietary choices in most countries. If you plan well balanced meals, nothing he needs for complete stamina will elude him. If you forget to respect singularity with food, you set the stage for forgetting in others. This is the beginning of rebellious behavior.

It isn't difficult to understand why. To make it

clear you only need to consider your own tastes. Some foods are welcome and some are not. Would you like someone forcing you to eat what you didn't enjoy? And if they kept at it, what would you do? Give your child the same freedom; the selection of what pleases his palette.

After you've allowed autonomy with choices, he'll challenge you for the right to eat what he loves in whatever way he wants to consume it. This is what you refer to as table manners. Isn't this really about you, not the child? Don't you have some emotional investment in his performing in a way you approve of, and if he doesn't, aren't you afraid someone else will disapprove of you?

Bickering about manners is unnecessary. If your child loves you, he'll copy you as soon as he's able to perform the maneuvers. If you give him a chance to enjoy the emulation, he will. And he'll do it with diligence and perseverance because he will love pleasing you.

If meals become a struggle with arguments and discomfort, why would he think you knew something important about it? He's instinctively anxious to copy you but it's about locating ease, not stress. When you create the latter, you're not going to find him receptive to your habits. It's no good to tell him something is right or correct because he still remembers this won't necessarily make him happy. He's using his instincts for guidance. When he gets into boring or uncomfortable situations, he makes noises until you get him out of it. If that doesn't work, he just starts concentrating on something else. He's looking for you to help him locate the pleasure and he believe what he feels inside, not what you say works.

If you're interested in your child learning how to eat with the manners you believe in, bring the manners you believe in to the dinner table. It's no good to tell him to be polite if you spend the entire meal criticizing him. This doesn't seem like polite behavior to him. Let him see how you believe well mannered people behave and show him how it makes your life happier. This is what will make your child think you have an habit worth emulating.

When you decide Earth looks like a valuable encounter, it's the movement into what you consider nourishment. Eating is your first reminder of this concept in matter. Therefore, the more welcome, satisfying and serene this function, the easier it is to consider everything else as the same support.

Help your child find this belief easily, so that other material gifts enter his universe with the honor he first gives to ingestion.

EATING IS A HABIT TO NOURISH THIS DREAM.
KEEP IT SERENE IF YOU WANT IT TO LOVE YOU.

CHAPTER 7

Sibling Rivalry

**CHERISH YOUR CHILDREN
FOR THEIR INDIVIDUALITY.
RIVALRY THRIVES ON COMPARISONS.**

***

Can "justice" ever find its true meaning for your children if they believe that when they finally look good to you, they'll have it? And what do you believe about their personalities that convinces you they aren't enough the way they are? If your progeny are experiencing rivalry at a ferocious pace, you can be sure they don't feel comfortable in your approval without excuses or apologies.

Children battle for attention when they don't receive it. And the reason the supremacy battle is so important is because they think the supply of love is limited; i.e., if one gets it, the other doesn't. Where do they get this idea? When they hear you say or feel you think, why can't you be more like your brother or sister? Why wouldn't they suspect something is missing if you'd like them to be more like another?

This subtle dissatisfaction can manifest from comparisons outside the family as well. This abuse can be even more painful. How can the child even try to rectify the situation in this kind of frustration? You've told him he doesn't measure up to a competitor outside the family unit. It's hard enough to feel less than another sibling, but at least this rival is family. How can a child deal with this kind of uncertainty? He tries harder to get your approval, that's how. And as nerve wracking as it is when a child responds to his resentments by disruptions and arguments, it's still healthier than keeping everything inside and pushing it into the unconscious. At least this way, he helps his body relax.

As the parent, you experience the result of your own destructive comparisons as each tries to become the one who meets your standards. The more you compare, the more you'll receive exasperation. It's your child's way of reminding you that however he is, is the way he longed to be. If it's fine with him why isn't it fine with you? You have the person you longed to be. He's brought what he needs for living the life he wants and it's just as legitimate a choice as yours. When you can welcome his preferences and let it enrich your life, your child will bask in approval and have no need to compete.

Put yourself in your child's place for a day and ask if the support he receives is filled with sanction or condemnation. Do you welcome what he considers important to his schedule, or do you demand he join whatever you're doing? Do you thank him for the kindnesses he brings you, or take for granted that he should serve you? Do you delight in whatever talents each enjoys, or do you rate them as lesser or greater? Is your mind open to the diversity of each child's abilities, or do you secretly hope they'll all be like you? Do you demonstrate that individuality is desirable by welcoming the variations in others, or do you make fun of different customs and other cultures? Do you welcome all your children when it's appropriate for all to participate, or do you single out one here and there as the worthy one to accompany you? Do you make light of their peculiarities like you hope others will do for you, or do you ridicule anything that strikes you as odd or different?

Your children will someday interact with the rest of the world. Whether they're able to find and maintain peace depends on whether they're able to do it at home. Are you showing them how it's accomplished?

If you come from a family where sibling rivalry occurred on a regular basis, ask why you either wanted vengeance or received it. Who was making you feel you weren't enough? You can be sure that whoever did, learned this behavior from their parents just like yours are learning it from you. But you don't have to perpetuate it if you find a better way.

The hopes and dreams of your children are individual, but their longing to spend time with you is shared. When backbiting and bickering is done in front of you or brought to your attention after the fact, someone is trying to tell you that the balance of friendship has swayed, entering a thought that's filled with partiality instead. Rethink what you're focusing on with these children and try to investigate how you've forgotten to value them equally.

How do you do this? Well, how would you like to be acknowledged? Is there something you do well but either it's taken for granted or ignored? And what if your family suddenly told you how much they appreciated it? How would you react? Wouldn't you want to share it even more?

Reading a list of affirmations isn't going to help you find the ones you need for your children. They're showing you every moment by how they live. You just need to remember they want the same recognition you seek.

When you bring them your personalized praise, they'll learn to praise each other. When you treasure their individuality, they'll welcome the diversity in everyone else. When you acknowledge their differences and applaud them for it, they'll commend the originality of everyone they know. Think of each child as a little gem complete within himself; sure of all that he needs, happy with all of his choices, and excited to find what can be done with all of them.

COMPETITION IS THE DESIRE

FOR MORE LOVE.

DON'T MAKE YOUR CHILD FIGHT FOR IT.

CHAPTER 8

Sharing

THE ONLY WAY TO FIND EVERYTHING
IS TO GIVE IT AWAY.

***

How do you teach your children that sharing won't cost them love? This is what you must convey if you hope to convince a young one it's desirable. It won't work if you say it's nice to do it. It won't work if you say it's polite. It won't work if you say they're bad if they don't. The only thing they care about is if they're still going to have fun if they do. So how do you teach them that sharing is welcome and if they try it, they'll reap the rewards of finding even more?

The toddler will want to see the visible proof that sharing is indeed profitable. When the opportunity arrives to demonstrate how this principle works, offer the child who's willing to test it, the reward God believes in. What does God believe in? He believes in sending you everything you mete out and more. So if the toddler is willing to share one toy, bring him four to make up for it. This is what will convince him it's a good practice.

This is how the universe works and he might as well learn it when he's young. What if he continues to think he'll receive if he shares? Wonderful... because he will. If you forget to reward him, some other God will. But the more you can be the one who does, the faster he's going to learn this axiom. If he realizes how exciting this process is, he's going to keep testing it wherever he goes. He may not receive the immediate response you give him, but the bonus will come nevertheless.

When he first leaves home to go to school, more opportunities will quickly manifest for testing this concept, and whether you're there or not, the universe will still be responding to his sharing aura.

If he questions that it doesn't seem to work so well in school, you can teach him how this theory varies in creativity. He'll want to understand how he's still gaining, even if he doesn't receive five crayons back for the one he gives away.

This is the time to explain that the gift back may have a different look, but it will still be something he loves. Ask him what happened after he gave his crayon away. He'll remember some little remuneration and realize his reward.

There will always be this bonus, so don't be timid about asking your child to remember it. God isn't forgetful about how to love himself. The mirror is always working. This game will intrigue your little one, and he'll keep testing it for however long he reaps the benefits.

Eventually, he's going to test it in the opposite direction and take something. Don't be upset. Just kindly explain that it's the same principle and because it works so well, it manifests regardless of what he metes out. If stealing is what he thinks he wants back, the universe will oblige that too. And for everything he robs from another, someone will come along and rob four times that, from him.

Don't be afraid of these wonderful precepts for your child. He's looking for them. It's what he came into humanness to find and if you're aware of what he's trying to understand, he'll find it all the sooner.

Take your child into your confidence. Reveal how this principle works in your own life. He'll be very curious to hear all your stories about how the universe read what you shared and sent you the same back and more. Even his own presence is a reflection of this. You told the universe you were ready to see more God in yourself and so God sent you more of himself in your child.

As your youngster moves into the primary school years, he's going to do a lot of testing with his peer group. Whether he has success with them or not is going to depend on his ability to enter open friendships. If he feels confident that he knows how to give of himself, friends will gather around him in droves. If he fears that he isn't enough, others who feel the same will find him.

Productivity begins the moment you step into matter and it accelerates when you produce what the universe loves to support. And since the only product that anyone is truly looking for is love, those who know how to give it are in demand.

The same tenet is working whatever age group you

refer to, but it's especially vivid in children. They haven't been distracted yet by the adult world that tells them to get, get, get, if they want to be popular and happy. Children don't care if someone is considered important because he has a lot of money, a big house, or a fancy car. If you don't believe this, just try to force your child to play with someone for this reason.

He wants to be with the playmate who gives him what he's looking for, regardless of his appearance, where he lives or how he got there. And what he's looking for is the friend who acts like God. What does God act like? He gives you whatever he has to share, whenever the need arises, with a friendly smile and a happy heart.

His need for this kind of friend never ends, but detours can come along that seem temporarily more attractive. It's just the testing that humanness is all about. How long he gets fooled depends on how long he's willing to ignore his inner longings.

If you want your child to be someone who understands the benefits of sharing, make sure you show him how it works for you. Let him participate in your conversations, and allow his respectful opinion to be heard. If you chat about a wonderful movie in front of him, but tell him he can't see it, he isn't going to think of you as much of a sharer, is he? Never mind that he wouldn't even enjoy the movie. That's irrelevant. What matters is that you're excited about something in front of him, but saying he can't enjoy it too. He feels resentment and anger, and the thought enters his heart that something he wants is being kept from him. He'll try to figure out why you would deny him your excitement.

Telling him he's too young is not a good reason. If he's too young to understand it, why would it matter if he went? Telling him the theater won't allow young children won't do either. The only gift he believes in is being with you in mutual fun, so if children aren't allowed in fun things, you're teaching him to expect lack. If he expects it he'll receive it, and this isn't what most parents hope for their children.

Learning about sharing happens at a very young age. Whether this situation is about a movie, a party, a conversation, or a vacation, if you tell your child he can't have the pleasure you're having, it's impossible for him to find joy in the concept.

What is the solution? It's to give your children the same respect you'd give anyone else visiting your home. Keep the conversation centered around thoughts that include everyone and are, therefore, enjoyable for all to think about.

Sharing is an explosive subject. The popular moral ethic says it's desirable, but most believe it really means giving up. Until you, as the parent, can realize how it opens up your own life, your child isn't going to believe it works.

Nevertheless, it's the only way you'll ever learn to truly know yourself. And the reason for this is because it's the process that puts your explosion into gear. In order to know who you are, you need to understand your energy, and when you're sharing it's easy to recognize. Why? Because the entity who gives of himself has unlocked the key to receivership and this is the feeling of abundance. In the feeling of abundance is the everything that life is. And once you've found it, you just keep on receiving more of this everything.

That's why children have an easy time finding playmates they feel comfortable with. They just go into automatic pilot towards the energy that feels good to them. They don't allow any other interference to destroy what they know they like. They value what's comfortable, so whatever and whoever doesn't fall into this category is left behind.

This same single mindedness can be relearned through the example of your children. Watch how they move from thought to thought, always opting for the entertaining direction and the jovial playmate. Then try to follow their example.

Your child will try to activate your imagination into the game of choosing comfort. If you are receptive, you'll have a lot of good times together.

If you preach to share with others, but don't know how to share yourself with the child, you aren't going to find success with your directives. The most precious sharing thought in your child's imagination is connected to his reunion with you. One of the reasons he came into humanness was because he believed in what he'd find through your love. Before he arrived, he understood your heart very well. You don't need to hide anything from him. Whoever you are is who he wanted. Open up to let him in. Honor his need to be with you. If you hadn't needed his beauty too, you wouldn't be together.

Keep mindful of how you felt as a child and how excited you were to learn about your parents. You waited for every detail, didn't you, savoring whatever they were able to give of themselves. You didn't care if they'd made mistakes. In fact, it was exciting to hear how they'd learned through trial and error.

Perhaps there's still a longing to connect up to your own dear parents with sharing. Did you miss a closeness you always dreamed was supposed to happen? Did you try to pretend you had it anyway? Did you tell your friends it was around even if it wasn't? Did you play games where the endings came out differently?

How can you mend from this hurt so your children gain from what you didn't have? If you could bring these entities back into your life in the same capacity and ask them to love you differently, what would you want them to do?

Listen to you more? Hug you more? Play sports with you, think up games together, go on trips together, respect your privacy, honor your friends, or maybe leave you alone more? What was left undone? What feels incomplete? Where is the ache?

Believe it or not, you can fill this gap. It doesn't heal from ignoring what happened. It doesn't heal from pretending it didn't. It heals from giving away what you never received.

Look at your children as the chance to rebirth into all the experiences you missed. They'll participate with more enthusiasm than you can ever dreamed of your parents offering. They'll return the love with more cherishing than your parents understood. They'll think up new games to embrace your caring tenderness. And they'll invent compassion where you never knew it existed.

Give them what you didn't have. Exist in the openness you yearned for. Then you won't remember the loss of what didn't manifest in your own childhood. The sharing of "now" will be all that matters.

YOU ONLY RECEIVE
WHAT THE UNIVERSE WATCHES YOU SHARE.
THEREFORE, IF YOU KNOW EVERYTHING IS YOURS,
IT IS.

CHAPTER 9

Discovering The Body

BEFORE YOU CAN HAVE THE FULLNESS
OF LIFE,
YOU MUST DISCOVER
THE ABUNDANCE OF YOUR BODY.

***

The infant believes his body is the universe. And what else would he surmise when all that he knows is how he feels? Gradually, he becomes aware of other things around him, but even so, he still only garners knowledge from what he's able to discern from his own inner senses.

This is the world he has just left—the existence where spirit knows its emotions are the source of its own enlightenment—so it takes a while for the baby to find any other reality.

When you're ready to leave humanness, the sensations you've found join what you call memory and become a part of your essence forever. The baby has embarked on this knowing journey for the sole purpose of garnering as many pleasurable impressions as possible. And he'll start investigating what they might be as soon as his coordination allows it.

If you want a happy child, encourage him to learn about his body. If he can appreciate it, it will return his love a thousand fold by finding the beauty in every function it performs.

The first performance he'll investigate involves his lungs; the miracle of sound. As he tests this beautiful new toy, he'll stretch it to the limits of his capacity because this is what he hopes to do with every nuance his body offers for research.

As he hears what he's able to generate through his vocal cords, all his other senses will clamor for attention too. For a while, they'll all seem miraculous for their newness. Until he takes them for granted the feeling behind each will thrill his very essence.

His sense of sight knows the beauty of everything; the eyesight of God in completeness. This miracle will last for a while and along with this, he also finds worldly vision. All will be bathed in colors and lights for some time, but it's still a pleasure of the body that's new to him.

He'll find plenty of practice with the next sense that involves his digestive system and this, of course, is eating. Exploration into this function is very pleasurable because it involves physical closeness to the nurturer. As he grows, what he finds in this arena can instigate a whole concept of living if he doesn't remember that it's just one of his many useful operatives; no more or less important than all the rest. Food is the very basis of continuity, until the soul understands eternity. When there's distortion about its use, the use becomes destructive. To keep eating in balance with all other pleasures, it's essential to remember its created purpose; nourishment of the heavenly machine that enables spirit to visit matter. When the amount it receives is too great or too small, the body reflects this misshapen theory of totality.

The olfactory organs are key in his early sensations because they lead him to his first meal. His instincts are acutely tuned into the aroma of milk, so he'll naturally seek out this nourishment.

As he's versing himself in the act of consumption, he learns what it means to dispose of waste. The infant is very aware of this function. He notices the relief associated with it. He understands that it's healthy and normal because the comfort it brings is recognizable. Ease and peacefulness have been his companions for quite a while and will feel like old friends immediately. To be rid of what isn't needed is very comfortable, whenever it's happening.

The warmth he finds from the first embrace teaches him physical contact. Can I ever know such bliss again, is what he feels. And everything that follows will be to remind him of the love of this experience.

Discerning mobility begins with his reaching for whatever seems a worthy prize in front of him. This stimulation fascinates his imagination for hours. Discovering the joy of texture, shape, color and size, is a delightful pastime in his new environment.

Soon after he masters his early skills, he'll look for new challenges. All of them are important in terms of growth. The body offers marvelous ways to expand and he hopes to realize them soon. He doesn't want to miss anything. If you help him love what he's created, you'll find the same joy in his discoveries.

How can you help him savor all these sensations? By remembering that every one is a beautiful gift; by believing that all are the love of God, and therefore, worthy of adoration. By encouraging him to rejoice in what he learns about how they all function.

When children grow up with distorted views of normal bodily functions, it's because they agreed with a parent who believed something was wrong with being human. Being human is a miracle in matter and whatever it offers is the love of God. If the essence called "everything" didn't think a sensation was important, you wouldn't have it. Treasure the beauty that expresses itself with your children in whatever area of their bodies they're discovering, and be glad that the caring love they believe in is here to learn with you.

The newborn is delirious with joy when he first comes into humanness because he can't feel anything uncomfortable. When he's hungry you feed him. When he's wet you change him. When he laughs you praise him. When he cries you comfort him. During this time when his every wish is fulfilled, humanness doesn't feel any different from the transition he just left. Therefore, he believes he's still in heaven with a few more sensations to enjoy. If he never had any reason to stop thinking he was in this blissful state of complete satisfaction, he would never leave it. And all the new sensations would become a part of the glorious happiness he already knew.

Why does he leave the conviction that to be on Earth is the same Garden of Eden he just left? He hears an idea that says something is wrong, and he believes it. Frequently, these distortions begin with the parent's attitudes about the body. He comes ready to remember that wondrous offerings are to be found. When he hears differently it causes confusion. The discrepancy between his belief and his parent's often falls into the categories of tactile, oral, or disposal sensations; always appearing as a lack of approval for how the child is enjoying them.

Why wouldn't he be curious? Aren't you curious when something new happens to you? Everything the child finds is exciting; a wonderful world of new discoveries in sight, sound, and texture. Why would he have judgments on any of it? He couldn't wait to get here to bring his cherished dream into form and he wanted to enjoy every phase of unearthing this gold mine of himself.

The body and everything it does is a source of pleasure for every human at every stage of his life, but never is there more enthusiasm for the pure newness of it all than when the child first realizes his own ability to be completely self-sufficient. He finds this wonderful little machine that can eat, sleep, eliminate, excite, see, smell, hear and touch all by itself. What could there be in toy land that was more interesting than this?

Be attentive to your little one's rebirth into

expansion. Let him explore without condemnation. Appropriate behavior isn't something you have to force on anyone, let alone a child. Each finds his own path for conformity as he grows. Because spirit always heads instinctively for the comfortable posture, you won't have to do any preaching about seeming deportment.

Games between youngsters to explore the body occur as a result of curiosity. Does everyone look like me? Do girls look different from boys? Does everyone feel the same sensations? Recognize a curious God when you see one. Try to remember how you investigate whatever stimulates you. Welcome his inquisitiveness and share all that he's begging to understand. Don't worry about questions that might be too advanced. He'll only ask what he's able to comprehend.

The body is a miracle created by Gods who want to make their repertoire of knowledge unlimited. Every gift it holds is expressed through the bodily senses that consume it. Whenever you help your child love what he can do, delight in what he finds, and love what he can be, all that he is, grows.

CHILDREN BEGIN HUMANNESS
WITH THE ONLY GADGET
THAT TRULY FASCINATES THEM,
AND WHEN YOU THINK OF WHAT IT CAN DO,
IT'S NO WONDER.

CHAPTER 10

The Questioning Child

**QUESTIONS ARE LIKE THE MORNING SUN.
THEY FILL THE PANORAMA WITH LIGHT.**

***

Love comes into your heart through a beam of heavenly brilliance that accesses through your aura. And the way your aura allows this light beam entrance could be termed a question. It's the opening that makes it all happen because pondering is what makes room for new thought.

Your child has so much he wants to learn that his aura is literally bursting with questions. The second he's able to articulate them, he'll begin. Each time you give him an answer that stimulates his imagination for more questions, his heart is illuminating with light filled thoughts that lead a pathway to heaven.

Don't judge his inquiries as he pursues whatever seems interesting. You can be sure that whatever subject activates his curiosity is meaningful to him. Sometimes a parent thinks he'll go crazy as his child finds something to query concerning every detail of existence. But if you articulate your answer in a manner that respects and honors his intelligence, the inquiries he comes up with will reflect your consideration.

Think of how you'd feel if suddenly you were transported to a new planet. Wouldn't you be bursting with wonderment about how everything worked and who was with you? This is how your child feels and he can't hold it in. Listen carefully to what he asks you, letting him sense your desire to help him grasp the meaning of whatever he longs to comprehend.

If on occasion you don't know the answer, let him see that you don't. Assure him you're not the least hesitant to seek the information elsewhere. This is what teaches him that everyone is here to learn together and finding answers is a happy and useful endeavor.

If you bluff your way through, fearing he won't love you as much because you don't have the solution at your fingertips, he doesn't learn anything except how to deny himself help. Eventually he'll find his answers, and if you tried to fool him, he won't love you for it. He'll just stop thinking you have any solutions for him.

Questioning isn't something that stops as childhood ends. It's a lifelong occupation because energy is always pondering what will love it more. And the more serene this sharing starts out with you, the better equipped your child will be for the later challenges.

If you find yourself with a youngster who never stops talking and repeats himself over and over with the same demands for knowledge, interaction between the two of you is off balance. The constant chatter with very little meaning behind it, is your cue that he's receiving the same from you; lots of words with very little content in them.

To heal this misalignment is to respond to what he's really asking; do you have time for me? Don't try to fool him by pretending it's his problem. Two light beings who come together to grow don't believe that only one has an opportunity. Receive the love this situation offers and evaluate whether you know how to give what he needs. If you can, it's the gift you give to yourself. As you look for the perfect alignment with him, this is what your soul feels as well.

Even in the early stages of childhood, the baby is questioning you for leadership. The absence of words doesn't mean his soul isn't searching. He peers into your aura with determination for guidance and reads what you believe in. If he doesn't agree with what he finds, his little body squirms in discomfort. Bring reassurance that you find him miraculous if you want him to trust your opinions and feel comfortable in your aura.

The body is made up of atoms which go through extraordinary explosion in the early years. How frequently they expand and in what category, is an ever changing phenomenon. Just as your body stays healthy and strong from food you love and exercise that's pleasurable, so does the mind expand from the stimulation that excites it.

When you use your muscles in a sport, the body starts exploding muscle atoms to make the endeavor more fun and challenging. If you start using your questioning faculties, these atoms start exploding too. And these atoms stimulate growth just as surely as the muscle growth manifests.

Atoms start dividing and splitting at a ferocious pace and every time they do, more space is available for more exploding. It never stops because you never stop growing, but the rate at which you do is very flexible.

If you want your children to enjoy their own personal explosion to the fullest, facilitate it with your own belief in their questioning resonance. Stay tuned into their curiosities about life, love and the dream for serenity, and then when they find it you'll be enjoying your own.

**THE LIGHT YOU HOPE YOUR
CHILDREN BECOME
BEGINS WITH THEIR CURIOSITY.**

CHAPTER 11

Anger/Fear

IS IT REALLY DANGEROUS
TO EXPERIMENT WITH IDEAS?
IF YOUR CHILD THINKS IT IS,
HE'LL FEEL FEARFUL.

***

As God leaves infancy to become more fully realized, his joy expands proportionately to the comfort he grows up in. If you offer him opportunities to broaden horizons with confidence and support, he'll begin these challenges with happy expectancy. On the other hand, if he meets with poisonous predictions about his search for independence, he'll approach the future with fear and trepidation. The child may eventually overcome a pessimistic indoctrination, and if he's chosen parents who propose this challenge, he believes it's helpful in the long run. But if you're a doubter who finds difficulty imagining a future filled with safety, you can give him a short cut right now by rethinking what is dangerous and what isn't.

To be alive in the matter world is not dangerous. It is, instead, the game of choice your child believes will lead him to a fuller understanding of his beauty. If you tell him he'll face all kinds of terrible people and all manner of dishonesty, he's going to have a hard time remembering how happy he was to come.

He will also lose faith in you. It isn't that he dislikes you for telling him these things so much as it is that deep down inside he knows it isn't true. No one would choose to come to a place filled with horrors and misery, and your child isn't going to think this poorly of himself.

As he matures, if he's able to break away from your philosophy to find his own, he'll be reaping the rewards of autonomy. If he can't, he'll assume the same self-hate you have and continue to demean his encounter. But you won't benefit from his inability to leave your aura, because whenever a person demeans himself he does the same to everyone around him. All that he has ahead of him is filled with whatever he puts into it. If you remind him of this, he'll believe you're a very wise parent.

There are some pitfalls children can run into, especially when they're just beginning to take a good look at their surroundings. But just because they exist doesn't mean your child has to associate fear with them. Common sense is what they're about. And when you forget to live with sanity in every category, fear has a chance to erode your experience.

Early on in his inquisitiveness, he'll start investigating closets, boxes, nooks and crannies, looking for hidden treasures of discovery. He can't help doing this. It isn't bad or naughty or even undesirable. It's just the curiosity that God has about any idea he enters. To discourage a child from researching his surroundings is not supportive. Take into consideration the fun you have when visiting a new location, and how curious you are to look around at everything it offers.

This is how your child feels. He doesn't want to miss a thing. It seems obvious to propose keeping things out of reach that are inappropriate for his investigation, but it's the only common sense answer there is. If the preparation has been overlooked and your exploring child gets into trouble, start your common sense approach instantly by forgetting about reproach and going into action. Whether it's helping him regurgitate or calling the paramedics, your decision to act will dissipate fear. When fear is gone, constructive emotions take over.

New challenges will consume this questioning God all along the path of his life. The strength of his limbs will become of interest as physical feats titillate his imagination. This is another juncture where either encouragement or fear can dominate. Don't judge what he's able to accomplish by what you could do. His communication with the ground is very keen when young. Therefore, he has a better sense of how far he can push himself.

Instead of warning him about how he's going to hurt himself if he keeps up whatever he's doing, praise him for how well he understands his body and knows how far he can take it. This way, if he takes a fall, he immediately remembers it's his judgement at stake, not yours. This is the beginning of recognizing responsibility.

Telling your child an activity is dangerous isn't enough to keep him from trying it. He's already seen he can do things you can't just because his body is so limber. When you believe some feat is unsafe, why not tell him there is no gain. He's more likely to hear this reasoning because he's looking for what makes sense.

Where is the wisdom that will make my life run smoothly, is the thought he'll connect up to. And your way of presenting this gift comes every day as you make your life the wisdom you believe in. If you encourage responsibility and common sense decisions, your child has a head start towards love. This is a quality God is very familiar with.

Your youngster wants to understand the difference between independence and foolhardiness. Naturally, he won't always have good judgement about what's safe and what isn't. He's just come from a place where everything is safe, whatever it is. He needs your guidance, not your ridicule of his judgement. When he shows an obvious need for leadership, show him what this quality is. Share that while his idea is interesting, there are lots of other possibilities and perhaps another might be more appropriate for the moment. The beauty in the way you do this is what teaches the child, not the circumstance that produces the debate.

How do you put this theory of common sense versus fear into practice when your toddler must understand the consequences of not following your advice? The explanation doesn't have to be filled with fear and punishment to be effective, it just has to be vivid enough for the child to get the point. Take the toys he relates to and reenact whatever scene you're trying to help him with so he comprehends what you're telling him. Don't worry if he's old enough to understand. He's always ready to hear explanations about anything he's ready to try.

As he attempts what fascinates him, give him your encouragement. That doesn't mean telling him to jump off a ten foot wall just because he's contemplating it. It means agreeing that the jump is indeed very daring and bold ideas have lots of growth. But if he tries it before he's taught himself how to take the fall safely, pain is the teacher he's looking for. At the same time, you can share that it isn't the only teacher, and he can enjoy this feat with skills if he first jumps off a low wall and learns how to fill the activity with pleasure.

Don't come up with lies to convince him of anything. All you'll do is convince him of your own ignorance. Children can feel when you aren't telling the truth and they'll begin to mistrust your advice as soon as they catch you mistrusting their intuitiveness.

Children learn very early how to calculate your integrity. They're sensitive to this knowledge because they still have the trusting aura of the God they were born as. Don't underestimate their insight if you want mutual trust to prosper and develop.

If common sense can overrule panic even with very young children, what is there to fear? God can't find anything that fits into this category. He sees every event as a learning tool. How safe is it for your children to learn on Earth? As safe as God's loving support system can be.

If your children determine that nothing is to be feared, only respected, this is how they feel about themselves. If they learn that every event teaches them an idea they're looking for, they'll look forward to what their life will manifest. If they learn that others are just as interested in finding common sense as they are, they'll welcome all who arrive as the support they're looking for. If they see you as a person who believes in their wisdom, they'll trust you as a God worthy of respect.

There aren't any fearful events transpiring. Circumstances only feel apprehensive when you forget they're welcome. Isn't it the worry that something's wrong that makes you edgy? Nothing is ever going wrong, because God is learning to love himself with whatever occurs. Show him you believe in him from the very beginning, and your life will reflect the wisdom of God.

DANGER IS THE IDEA
THAT YOU AREN'T IN A LOVING UNIVERSE.
FEAR IS WHAT HAPPENS TO YOUR SOUL
WHEN YOU BELIEVE IT.

CHAPTER 12

Discipline

TO ALLOW HEAVEN TO BE HELD
IN YOUR FUTURE,
YOU MUST UNDERSTAND
WHAT HEAVEN FEELS LIKE NOW.

***

Can you redefine the term discipline so that it represents what your child learns about himself, not what he learns about your demands?

His hope is to be deeply involved in some activity that tickles his fancy, but it doesn't help him find that direction if you insist he be disciplined about your inclinations. When he discovers his true talents, you won't have to force him to concentrate, he'll be full of enthusiasm without a word from you.

The only reason discipline is valuable is for how it helps you find you Godhood. Your child doesn't develop it for your sake, but for the eternity of his own soul. If you try to make his life disciplined for the ideas you believe in and disregard the ones that matter to him, all that he hoped to gain from being here is put on hold as he learns about resentment.

How do you teach him the value of discipline? You watch for what he loves to do. And when you see his fledgling talents, you encourage him to notice what happens if he uses discipline to develop them.

Isn't this what commitment is all about; making time in your life for what's important, developing abilities for fun and enjoyment, and learning to use your hours constructively so the whole works together in unison?

What if discipline isn't about restriction, but about expansion. Then, unless you can join this interpretation, you're going to have difficulty helping your children find it.

How do you know when it's loving to encourage something? When the child shows enthusiasm to pursue it. What about the youngster who has musical ability, but refuses to honor it with disciplined study? What about it? If he doesn't honor it, why should you? To force a child to spend hours practicing when he'd rather be doing something else, isn't what will teach him to love it.

If you've heard famous piano players or the like profess they wouldn't be where they are if their parents hadn't forced them to practice, take a better look at what really happened.

A child who senses a great deal of ability will feel proud of how well he progresses. If he finds it difficult to focus on studying, he may unconsciously ask his parents to help him. But you won't find long haranguing arguments concerning this issue. More than likely, it will be gentle nudging; God's little reminder that he considered this talent important for his happiness, so why not see it through to whatever it can bring him.

The time to step back and consider if this prodding is helpful is when the emotional contact between the two of you begins to lose it's loving essence. The child who knows that something else is more important will fight like crazy for his goal. The child who instinctively knows that practice is a blessing will acquiesce easily.

As you raise your offspring, more than likely he'll tell you what he loves if the atmosphere is open for sharing. Be excited and encourage him to test his passions, whatever they are. If he has several, let him try them all without reminders of how he dropped the last one. Haven't you experimented with lots of possibilities in order to find the ones you love the most?

If you make all kinds of rules and regulations because you think this will teach him discipline, just make sure you have a good reason for each. And just pleasing you isn't going to do the trick. There has to be some payoff for the child if his reasonable mind is to accept them. If there isn't, he won't be learning about discipline, he'll be learning about tyranny.

Discipline is something that each person learns from within as they find what captures their imagination. You can't force another to have it, but you can show them what it's done for you. Let him watch how you expanded a talent from the caring devotion you brought to it, and he'll have the teacher he longed for.

Think for a moment what everyone is searching

for. Isn't the goal for a good life where's there's pleasure and kindness; where each person can express himself individually and contribute to the whole? And unless your child can find what he loves and have the discipline to expand it, he isn't going to treasure his divinity the way he hoped to.

He has to learn to love who he is, not who you think he should be. He has the beauty of God within his soul, and he'll wake up to it when he sees this God in himself.

If you can be a constant reminder to respect his own individuality, you're being the parent he longs to know. This is the discipline of God; the willingness to love all that your are and to know it's enough.

PRESSURE TO CONFORM IS NOT
DISCIPLINE.
DISCIPLINE MANIFESTS WHEN THE CHILD
UNDERSTANDS HIS OWN DIRECTION.

Ridicule From Others

**HATRED COMES FROM THE INABILITY TO LOVE.
ITS CURE IS FORGIVENESS.**

***

Does this sound familiar? Could it be you've heard it before, just stated a little differently? What if you won't ever live anywhere, any place, where this phrase won't follow you? And if this is true would you be willing to look at it now? Because until you can, completion will always be an idea away from your precious heart.

If your child has been born into a caring, devoted family where each person lovingly supports the other, his instincts to overcome hatred will be strong. Nevertheless, he will find ways to strengthen whatever positive convictions he has so far.

A youngster who has never had any reason to mistrust or hate within the home, will most likely find his first challenge when he encounters other children. And since hatred only emerges when a person thinks he's different from others or left out from where he wants to belong, he will begin to hate the person who makes him worry.

Thus, the classroom situation where one seems different or unusual, and the other, not having the skills for embracing the diversity of choices, ridicules in an effort to feel more secure about his own.

Why does he feel more secure from ridiculing? Because he listens to this voice inside that says if someone is different, they aren't okay. And if he can divert the focus of dissimilarity to another, he thinks he'll feel more comfortable about himself.

Sooner or later, your child is going to be on both ends of this predicament. How you react is going to make a big difference in how fast he moves through it.

How do you comfort a little one when he has been discriminated against simply because he looks different, acts different, or talks different? How do you handle his pain and heartache as others make him feel out of place?

The first insight is to change your mind that anyone is to blame for what's happening. If you don't point the finger at the other children as being nasty and unkind, your child won't have to deal with reprisals. That's one big load off his mind immediately.

Secondly, if you take him lovingly into your arms and tell him how much you enjoy his individuality, he's going to stop thinking something is wrong with him pretty fast.

Thirdly, it's entirely possible to help this child reason through why the ridicule came in the first place. What was featured as different isn't as important as now the child learns to deal with it. Sometimes youngsters gang up against another because they're jealous. Sometimes because they're fearful. Sometimes because they're confused. But never because they're loved. If you can help your child understand the reason he was singled out, he has ammunition to counter it. And the most powerful ammunition that anyone can ever embrace is positive feedback.

In truth there is power. If your child has some physical abnormality, the kindest and most loving gift you can give him is your willingness to accept it wholeheartedly. This is what enables him to do the same. And if he can, his friends will be able to too.

Let's say he's been through some disfiguring surgery and because of it he feels embarrassed about his image. The sooner he can laugh and joke about what he's chosen to accompany him, the sooner he frees up his friends to do the same. If they call him funny face, he can agree with them without resentment. This is what ends ridicule.

If the person who is the object of abuse, freely admits there is humor in how he presents himself, he finds fans not fanatics. Who are the most endearing people you know? Those who can laugh at themselves, and thereby help you to do the same.

If you take sides, involve the teachers, include the parents, and generally make a stink, do you really envision this helping your child find acceptance? All this does is add flame to the fire and instead of his psyche undergoing a slight singe, he finds major searing.

Revenge won't fix the situation and that's what your child is hoping to understand. He wants to make a place for himself in his peer group—have friends and companionship—not create upset with classmates, teachers, and other parents. And he isn't searching for obligatory courtesy out of fear of retribution.

If the ridiculing children receive your child's desire to share whoever he is in whatever way he's able to with honesty and openness for his differences, a common ground is found. Why? Because the ridiculing barriers only come up when the other children see him as separate and different. When they receive the frank sharing of what is there for all to see—fear, doubt and mistrust are gone.

This predicament doesn't have to involve anything as obvious as physical differences to pop up in classroom and playground situations. It can be about the way a child combs his hair, walks, or maybe even just because he's new. But the solution is the same if you want your child to grow in loving feelings.

If you propose revenge and retribution, your child may make his point about being the butt of ridicule, but he won't have gained any skills towards peace in his life.

How do you deal with the youngster who leads this cruelty against others? Actually, he's facing the same demons; am I okay the way I am? Admonishing and lecturing will fall on deaf ears if your child is taking the stand that to become "fine" himself he must make another "not fine." He sees his peers as deserving of his courtesy when he sees himself as deserving of the same.

Ask how you treat this child. Do you give him all the love and honor he warrants? Do you reassure him that whoever he is, is fine with you? Does he find it easy to bring his hurts and pains to you? He'll only look to minimize others when he's not so sure he measures up.

Take this sweet adorable God into your arms tonight and tell him how much you love him. Speak with words that bring him reassurance of his worthiness. Remind him that the tenderness in him is truly beautiful and you love the many delights he brings into your life. A child who receives this kind of reinforcement won't be a bully for long. He'll be too interested in bringing the same nourishment to others.

Your home is the breeding ground of behavior and all your attitudes will be under scrutiny from your children. When you receive abuse from another, how do you handle it? Do you forgive and move one, or do you harangue for days about the dirty rotten lout who couldn't keep his mouth shut? If someone teases you, can you look at yourself and find humor, or do you look for the moment you can avenge yourself and stab him in the back?

When you show your child what you believe works, he's going to try whatever it is. He might decide it doesn't work too well and go his own way, but you have the opportunity of showing him what you hope for his life by what you bring to yours.

Forgiveness doesn't mean letting yourself become the object of abuse. It means finding the compassion to remember that criticism and mistreatment only come from those who receive the same. It means recognizing how situations only come into your aura if they have something important to show you about your own behavior. It means taking responsibility for all that you manifest and leaving blame in the trash can, where all unusables belong.

This is how your child learns to withstand the traumas that find their way into everyone's experience. And when he takes the position that careful insight is what turns the situation around, he won't be investigating how to handle abuse, he'll be learning how to deal with miracles.

**YOUR CHILD PUTS HIMSELF
THROUGH RIDICULE
WHEN HE CAN'T FIND HIS WORTHINESS.
SHOW HIM HOW WORTHY HE IS
BY KNOWING YOUR OWN.**

CHAPTER 14

Allowance And Chores

BOTH OF THESE CONCEPTS
FIND FRUITION IN HARMONY
WHEN YOUR CHILD SEES HIMSELF
AS A PART OF THE WORKING WHOLE.

***

Children have the amount of insight from chores that they allow themselves from helping you. If they view their existence as a beautiful contribution to the family unit, they'll take pride in their achievements. If they see themselves as a slave to your whims, they'll feel alienated.

A chores is the excuse for teaching the idea of pulling together. If it isn't teaching this, ask what it's supposed to accomplish. It won't teach discipline unless the child enjoys his task. It won't teach respect unless he feels pride in the household. It won't teach the loving aspects of participation unless you're working right alongside him.

When a family has many members and the work must be divided in order to make living together run smoothly, children will find chores delightful. They may complain now and then when they want to do something else, but if everyone is pulling their share, the child who is asked to help will feel enfolded in the group, and therefore loved.

If you use his strength and youth to do hard labor just because he's living under the same roof, he'll constantly challenge your right to barter on his health and agility. He'll want to know what he's supposed to gain. If there is no payoff, rebellion and unpleasantness will follow. In this situation, allowance often enters the scenario.

Offer him the chance to learn what chores are about before you teach him that helping around the house is a job. If he grows up believing that payment must come for his contribution, he won't help unless he's always receiving. I'll clean my room if you'll take me to the Mall, just becomes, I'll fix the closet if you'll give me sex, later in life. Chores are the natural outcome of households that work together in harmony. They aren't trade-offs for favors.

As children develop skills, there's nothing harmful about showing them in a financial way that you value their talent. To assist a loved one as he supports himself with a gift, is a beautiful thought. There's a big difference, however, between paying your daughter to make a dress for you as she perfects her seamstress skills, and giving her money to keep her room clean.

Allowance can be volatile subject because the children can't agree with the parents about what it's for. Even parents have difficulty agreeing among themselves. It makes sense that young children need money to purchase what pleases them, but what amount is fair for both parties?

Why not ask your child what he thinks? Believe it or not, when he's trusted to come up with an equitable amount, he'll want to show you how wise he is. You'll probably find his amount very logical and well conceived.

If he spends it on what you think is wrong, let him. It's his to do whatever he wants with. Unless he experiments with how long it will last, he won't learn how to manage it. Make him responsible for what becomes of it and he'll take more of an interest in what he does with it.

Children who grow up in a household where they must contribute to the income to survive as a family, have a wonderful opportunity to gain self-respect. Think what a high it is to know that your parents consider you an adult and, therefore, able to bring what is needed into the family unit. To help those you love in such a tangible way, fosters enormous generosity as the years progress. In this instance, chores take on the nature of yearly wages for a family. This makes a child feel important and needed. This is what fosters worthiness.

Allowance exists for those who haven't reached the age of earning. If your child continues to receive after this, he won't have much incentive for creating funds in other ways. Even though you feel generous as you give, if he believes his livelihood depends on you instead of himself, a deep underlying resentment can develop. Your greatest gift is to show him what independence brings. Put responsibility where it belongs; into the hands of the entity who wants to become self-reliant.

When wealthy families share their bountiful income with relatives and children, allowance takes on a whole new definition. For offspring of those who leave behind a fortune, self-reliance becomes, how to find one's own identity regardless of what achievements preceded you. This is still a challenging and worthy game and God finds his beauty through it many times. It creates a new set of standards where survival becomes the ability to differentiate between fortune in terms of money and fortune in terms of eternity. However, the principle remains the same; a way to help that person have fun with material things until he learns how to achieve this on his own.

The happy ending is the unveiling of God in his dominion of everything. Whatever teaches this concept is the true gift of love. Let this be your guide as you contemplate how to raise your children.

Am I teaching them what it means to be self-expressed? Am I encouraging their confidence? Am I putting my faith in their wisdom? Am I remembering they have their own perception of knowingness? When you embrace these thoughts for the education of your children, you can't stray far from the love of God.

ALLOWANCE IS THE CHILD'S PRIZE
AS HE TRIES TO HAVE FUN WITH MONEY.
CHORES ARE HIS REWARD FOR BELONGING.

CHAPTER 15

Homework

THE HOMEWORK OF SCHOOL
JUST GETS YOU READY
FOR THE HOMEWORK OF LIFE.

***

School is a training ground, where hopefully you gain insight into habits that will release productivity when you leave. Homework is just one of the many tools for encouraging this constructive output. It's designed for gaining knowledge, learning study habits, planning time, and feeling a sense of achievement. When you participate, ask if this is what you're helping your child do.

If you care desperately that your youngster achieves, it's time for a look at yourself, not him. What he learns in his early training starts him off in a direction that either propels him into self confidence or self-defeatism. If you have one in the latter category, ask how he could have gotten the idea that he isn't enough. When a child knows his accomplishments are more important to his parents that his personal happiness, he will feel lonely and defeated.

Striving, striving, striving for your youngster to shine, to be the first and the best, to reflect on your intelligence as the parent of such a glittering beacon of brilliance is a sorry initiative to perpetuate. And more importantly, it won't work.

What it will create is the mutinous progeny who refuses to follow your dictates, or a little one who escapes your aspirations by turning inward into his own private world of sanity, or the child who lies, cheats, and tries anything to accomplish what he knows you think is important. But it won't create this shining, glittering beacon of love you're so hopeful of molding.

Homework is a very intelligent use of instruction if realistically designed to the abilities of its students. Its primary value is to show that time set aside to reach a prideful goal will achieve results. Whether he remembers the capital of every state or the name of every river is insignificant in the long run. But if he learns that information is found from purposeful study, he'll still be using this knowledge long after third grade.

School isn't about how many facts your child can cram into his mind. It's about learning to ingest information in a loving manner; welcoming new ideas with sensitivity, finding enthusiasm for new ways of doing things, and fostering inquisitiveness for expansion.

Look at the big picture of your child's life. Can you truly believe that skills for memorizing will make it more rewarding than the acquired art of relishing enthusiasm for learning? This is what homework can do for him; teach him how to find information on his own and feel the accomplishment of independent scholarship.

If his school doesn't understand this concept, teach him yourself. When enough students know what they're looking for, the teachers will reflect the new emerging theories.

To be educated is to know yourself. School is no different from other learning situations you choose along the path of your life. If for you, scholarliness is what will make your own days more pleasant, go for it, but don't judge that this as what your child necessarily needs for serenity. Let him investigate whatever achievement is comfortable. This is the education that's vital.

How do you relate to what your child brings home from school? Do you take charge of his lessons? Do you organize his afternoon and evening, designating how he must allot his time? Do you insist on seeing what he has accomplished? Do you grade it before it's turned in? Do you demean his effort and try to shame him into working harder? Do you worry that he isn't the student you hoped he would be? Do you lament his supposed shortcomings with your friends?

The child understands your attitude about each of these issues whether he's present or not. And if he feels your dissatisfaction, he'll begin to mistrust that he's fine with whatever abilities he does have. This is how you create the under achiever, not the over achiever. This is how you make sure he doesn't believe in himself. This is how you crush his desire to investigate individuality, by intimidating him into thinking he can't manage his own life.

To encourage the appearance of this genius you dream of him being, get behind him wholeheartedly in whatever he takes a fancy to. If studies aren't his forte, look for what he's showing you that is. Let him organize his evening, his homework, and his recreation. Let him judge what's appropriate. Let him be responsible for the results of his own decisions. That doesn't mean you can't assist, but the help is always to inspire his trust within.

What if the home you're working on is your heart, and therefore, all that you encounter is just to bring you home to yourself? You go to the school called Earth and you do your homework in order to bring your totality back to where it belongs. So how could anyone else really help you? They can only show you how they found a way to do homework that was successful.

All that you behold on this matter plane is symbolic; here to encourage autonomy. Treat your child's adventure into homework the way you hope to encourage your own independence; full of adoration for the blessed ideas he wants to investigate and support for his choices.

HOMEWORK IS THE ENDEAVOR
TO REALIZE SELF ACKNOWLEDGEMENT,
WHATEVER HOME YOU WANT TO WORK TOWARDS.

Social Achievement / Artistic Achievement

THESE TWO RARELY GO TOGETHER IN CHILDHOOD BECAUSE THE FIRST IS PERFORMED FOR YOU, WHILE THE SECOND IS FOR THE CHILD.

***

Deep in the heart of every parent is the desire for their children to surpass them. Sometimes confusion about what this means, colors what is focused on. In an effort to make the youngster a winner, the nurturer can become something of a complainer about the social graces his child is willing to assimilate.

These amenities can make life run smoother, but the real reason you want your child to perform well has more to do with your self-esteem than his. What a wonderful parent everyone will think I am if my children are always polite, disciplined, and well versed in the basic social etiquette of my community. Can you deny that there isn't some of this justification as you move them into walking, talking, dressing, playing, sharing, reading, dancing, reciting, and polishing up on some musical instrument?

Many valuable contributions begin this way. However, there are limitations as to what any child can absorb and remain harmonious. If you become a dictator, demanding performance from your unwilling child, you won't create social graces. You'll create anger and resentment.

Most of his growth about manners comes from watching you, so make sure you act in a way that backs up your instructions. If you don't, you put yourself in an awkward position. To preach one thing and do another, puts him into confusion where he learns to pretend like you do. It turns you into a fool in his eyes; someone who makes one set of rules for himself and another for others. This won't go over big because the child wants to copy those he loves. When he's told he can't, he feels left out of your life even if it's about social amenities. This will encourage him to leave you out of his life, even if it's just about his social amenities.

A young child takes your point of view about everything, even how you feel about him. What do you suppose goes on inside his mind when you require too much too soon? Wouldn't he say to himself, something must be wrong with me if I can't remember what Mommy thinks is important. Maybe I'm dumb because I can't grasp what Daddy keeps telling me. Expecting a toddler to conform to adult behavior patterns before he even understands what they're for, gives him the clear message that he's a puppet to do your bidding. And when he can't make his mind and body perform to please you, he begins to doubt himself.

Why wouldn't he? That's what you must ask. Why

wouldn't he suspect he's less than he should be if he can't perform in a way that pleases you? You are his world. He anticipates that everyone will be like you. If you see him as inadequate—whether it's about saying thank you at the appropriate moment, or wetting his bed—he's sure to think the whole world believes the same.

Can't you remember when you were young and expected everyone you met to respond the same as your parents? Can't you remember the first time you realized that their attitudes weren't necessarily all pervasive?

Children don't learn to behave one way or another from your words. They learn from watching your behavior. Therefore, if you want your little one to grasp what's important to you, make sure you live what it is you're trying to teach.

If you want him to say thank you for every little gift that comes his way, show your gratitude for every little gift that comes to you. If you want him to practice his lessons with diligence, practice whatever contribution you value. If you want him to be an early achiever, concentrate on whatever it is you're trying to achieve. Don't worry if he'll catch on. When he sees you enjoying yourself, whatever it is you're doing, he'll want to copy you right away with whatever it is he's doing.

Children have a great deal to explore in their initial years. When they're constantly harangued about how they're behaving, how they're looking and how they're learning, pressure builds up in their psyches. Something is wrong, Mother isn't pleased. Something is amiss, Daddy is irritated. So they try harder to please you.

They'll compete for your attention in an effort to sense your approval with: look at this Mother, look at that, Daddy. Is this okay? Am I fine? Are you pleased? And anything that seems to have your okay more than they do, becomes their target; i.e., the telephone, the cooking, other children, office work, or whatever competes for your energy. If you want them to feel comfortable in other activities that please you, bring your pleasure to whatever they love.

When you wonder whether advice from others is sound, ask if your child will feel good about himself if it's introduced. If you sense he'll feel sad, uncomfortable, physically hurt, ashamed, morose, or guilty, it isn't productive regardless of who recommends it.

Sometimes the answer for comfort varies from child to child in the same family. What one might adore, the other could dread. Listen to each with an open heart so they don't feel left to your ambitions instead of their own.

Expanding talents is a worthy pursuit, but ask who your child is doing it for, you or himself. Children gain expertise easily about something they love if the seed of interest has been planted. But they are the planters of their own garden and know the flowers that will grow to maturity with ease. If you force them to plant hybrids when they only want daisies, the soil won't support growth.

Parents, in the desire to bring a full spectrum of interests into the youngster's aura, can forget to notice what is welcome. Make whatever you want available. Then sit back and let them choose what pleases them. To lovingly explore whatever artistic achievements will make their garden beautiful, is to willingly to let go of their accomplishments to please you, and relinquish it to their own ambitions.

Everyone entering the human plane brings some talent to enjoy. Each knows the degree of proficiency to bless his life. Whether he's highly skilled or moderately talented has no relevance to his happiness. He hopes to remember that he believed in the wisdom of what he brought.

Your contribution to this unveiling is to encourage whatever natural propensities reveal themselves early in life. It won't be hard to notice if you're open to whatever manifests. If you're dogmatic about what they should look like, both of you are going to feel frustrated.

Some children emerge victorious with individuality intact. Some can't find the strength for independence and follow in footsteps that don't feel comfortable. And in between there are many layers of self-reliance and many stages of rediscovery. But the detours aren't necessary. All can find their particular interests with ease if the atmosphere is filled with freedom to choose autonomously.

If you stay alert to the stimuli your child relates to and encourage whatever makes him happy, he'll find his talents with ease. And as he moves into accomplishments that are meaningful, he'll acquire the social graces of a happy person.

This is what will make you proud and happy because this is where the shining, glimmering beacon originates; from God finding the light that leads him home to love.

ACHIEVEMENT
IS THE ABILITY TO REALIZE AUTONOMY.
IF THIS IS WHAT YOUR CHILD
IS LEARNING,
HE'S ON A POWERFUL PATH.

CHAPTER 17

Adolescence

WHERE DO WE GO
FOR THE THINGS WE NEED?
TO THE PERSON WE BELIEVE HAS THEM.
SO WHEN YOUR TEENAGER BEGINS LOOKING
FOR WHAT IT MEANS TO BE A FREE SPIRIT,
MAKE SURE HE FINDS ONE WHEN HE TALKS WITH YOU.

***

Children reaching these years take on new adventures at a very fast pace. Whether they enjoy them or hate them can sometimes depend on how happily you accept their progress.

Risk takes on new meaning as the teenager rushes headlong into whatever seems challenging. How is your risk taking these days? Do you still believe extra effort is worth the reward, or have you settled for something less than you deserve?

His strength and agility are at an all time high and he revels in using his body to encourage stamina and power. Is your existence one of lethargy, where you've forgotten to stimulate your muscles and encourage cell rejuvenation?

He has an appetite that makes you wonder how he can consume so much and still maintain pleasing proportions. Are you in a rut where you've forgotten to listen to your own body rhythms as they tell you what nourishment is necessary for the amount of exertion that's comfortable?

He's full of brilliant concepts that make him feel like a genius, and he wants to share them with anyone who'll listen. Do you follow through when a direction sounds productive, or do you pooh pooh it with some negative self-denial?

He feels like the world is his oyster and wants to welcome everyone into his enthusiastic outlook. Have you kept your optimism or have you decided life is one big disappointment after another?

The opposite sex has suddenly become delicious to notice and new sensations are being discovered every day. Are you still appreciative of the varied delights that sexual attraction can bring into your experience, or have you gotten bitter and discouraged from enjoying this facet of life?

He develops individuality in his dress, music, hair, appetite and friends, and joins those who feel the same passions. Are you still pleasing yourself in all these categories or have you opted for the conformity that says, don't rock the boat?

He works his heart out for what he thinks is important and totally ignores what appears boring. Do you still give your attention to stimulating priorities, or have you compromised your time in areas of stagnant boredom?

He uses the premise that whatever he wants, he can get. Have you decided this is impossible and you'll never have what you want?

He can't imagine that each day won't have something fascinating to learn, and he's ready to explore it. As you approach each new day, are you primed for failure, or ready for excitement, fun, growing, learning and loving?

The only reason another irritates you is because you see something about them you want and don't think you can have. When you make sure that all these wonderful achievements are a part of your daily routine, you won't be irritated by your teenagers, you'll be inspired by them.

Besides all these healthy changes, the adolescent is suddenly adapting to a whole new set of emotions. For some, these highs and lows can precipitate fears that the body controls them instead of the opposite.

As all this growth burgeons forth, the urge to test newly found fortunes is extremely powerful. It really isn't that different from other stages of life when new options present themselves. But it can feel different to the parent who has forgotten to honor his own explorations. Suddenly he's reminded of his lost vitality, and the enthusiasm he sees in his children doesn't make him feel so good about himself. And in order to justify the loss of his own delight, he punishes his children for theirs. And the only means he sees for doing this is to discourage them from enjoying this new phase of growth.

When the knowing belief comes to the youngster that his parents don't welcome his adulthood, he has to take measures to prove that he is what he looks like. And how does he do this? He tries to assert his independence in whatever way his point can be made. The means are individual depending on what areas of growth the parents are most resistant to.

The solution is easy when you realize why the child behaves as he does. This isn't the time to tell him he can't be trusted to act like an adult. This is the time to welcome him in brotherhood as the same autonomous being.

This isn't the time to criticize his every decision in taste, it's the time to praise him for his individuality.

This isn't the time to wonder what he's doing in his leisure, this is the moment to remember he's using it to his best advantage.

This isn't the time to challenge his every belief, it's the moment to welcome whatever opinions he values.

This isn't the time to criticize his friends, it's the opportunity to welcome each and every one of them into your life.

The only basis for defiance is in the belief that there's someone to defy. If you're thrilled to welcome this young adult and give him the respect he deserves, why would he rebel? Nothing is going wrong when your teenager suddenly finds new intensities to submerge himself into. He's just exploring options. If you let him test the waters without making him feel intimidated and awkward, he'll pull through with enormous contributions to your life as well as his own.

When there's trouble brewing and you tell yourself

something has gone wrong with your child's direction apparatus, check out your own first. What have you told him about priorities by the way you live your own life. He won't respond to words as he begins to form his opinions, he'll notice what you live. And if he feels comfortable in your tenets, he won't have any reason to separate himself.

Be honest in all your shared experiences. This is how to encourage his honesty. Don't hide your feelings and he won't hide his. Don't judge what he deems important and he won't criticize your pleasures.

Make him feel that his ideas are significant, regardless of whether you share them; this teaches him tolerance for all those who disagree with him. Reassure him that whether he follows in your footsteps or not, you'll support whatever direction he favors.

Show him what it means to love yourself. This is his greatest longing. Honor what life means to you, and he will find his own interpretation that makes yours all the more enjoyable.

Bring compassion to your introspection as these children remind you what life is meant to be. This is a second chance to review where you've gotten off track. The insight is always in what riles you the most. Make this young adult the reflection that can seed your own rebirth into the priorities you left behind but still revere.

Let him take whatever course he loves without

backbiting comments, and you'll begin to respect whatever direction your life veers towards.

Give him freedom to pursue whatever his tastes dictate, and you'll wake up to the pleasures that give your life meaning.

Make him responsible for his schedule, trusting he's wise enough to direct it towards productivity. Then your own resourcefulness will begin to explode.

Believe his opinions have validity in his universe of creation, and you'll start trusting that yours have created the universe that pleases you.

Ask only that he respect and honor each member of the family in the same way he longs to be admired, and the emotions between all of you will reflect this interchange of courtesies.

Welcome his suggestions as he asks for more tolerance in his friendships, and you will begin to see the friendliness of those he's chosen.

Remember that your fondest hope was to know this God well as he made his plans to enter matter. All that he is, is all that you hoped he'd be. As you please his heart with your acceptance, everything about yourself becomes pleasing to you.

ADOLESCENCE
IS THE SPLITTING OF THE ATOM
AT ITS MOST EXPRESSIVE SPLENDOR.

CHAPTER 18

Peer Group Temptations

THE SOLIDITY YOU LONG FOR IN YOUR CHILDREN
IS THE OUTCOME OF YOUR FAITH
IN THEIR ABILITIES.
WHEN THEY GO IN A DIRECTION THAT SEEMS UNSAFE,
STAY STEADFAST FOR WHAT IS SAFE FOR YOU.

***

Peer group pressure begins the moment a child becomes aware of the company he's with. The only time this phase takes on ominous connotations is when you label it unwelcome. Everything your child finds is valuable. Whether or not you understand its importance, have faith he does. It's the only way you'll ever find peace because nothing he wants to experiment with will be denied him no matter what you do, say, think, or feel when you're with him.

Negative peer group pressure is what the youngster succumbs to when he isn't finding the acceptance and approval he wants for himself. He isn't sure of what he loves or what he doesn't. He is sure if he's lovable or if he isn't. He isn't sure if he needs to be different to be worthy, or whether he's fine the way he is. And in order to discover what is true, he begins exploring possibilities he thinks will make it clearer.

On the other hand, if he understands what he loves, why he loves it, and values the presence of it in his life, no one can persuade him to do things differently.

How does he get to feel so good about himself that he follows his own dictates and doesn't care what anyone else decides to pursue? He gets this way from testing his ideas, seeing what happens when he does, choosing for thoughts that bring his life pleasure, and discarding the ones that don't work. How can you help him achieve this? By giving him responsibility for his own life from the moment he starts making decisions.

The first principle in helping your child take control, whatever the issue, is to reassure him you believe he is the one who dictates every possibility. He is responsible if he wants to try something, and whatever manifests from his responsible decision is his creation too. Reiterate that he must live with whatever happens from whatever indulgence.

Just warning him that something is dangerous won't mean a thing. Youngsters try lots of things you consider dangerous and nothing happens at all. They don't scare easily unless they've seen the ravages of what another's behavior has created, and even this doesn't influence them infallibly.

If you leave yourself out of the issue and tell him he has the ability to choose what he considers important, he immediately moves into a position of autonomy. This is a very powerful aura from which to honor decisions. It immediately dissolves any testing for reasons of rebellion alone.

If peer pressure influences those who are insecure, make sure he feels secure with you. Barring no one is hurt by his decisions, tell him you'll back whatever he decrees, even if you don't agree. This may feel like too much freedom for your youngster, but it's this inability to trust his judgement that makes him want to test your loyalty. When it's clear that his behavior reflects his own autonomy and not yours, he'll begin to act like a responsible adult.

There is no other solution because ideas are out there for whoever wants them, and no matter what you do to protect your children from seeming danger, if they're determined to try something, they will.

They really aren't so different from you, are they? How do you react when a person says, don't do that, and you see others having a good time with it? Doesn't this just pique your interest? But when you know you'll be responsible for whatever a decision brings, you take more care in what you select.

The person who opts for destructive behavior from an autonomous position, knows he's just as autonomous to stop. Whatever happens, there's no one else to blame, is there? Those who love him the most have told him he is his own person, free to do whatever he wants with his gift of life.

If he makes choices without mutiny in mind, he'll stop for himself if it doesn't go well. But if he turns masochistic as a means of getting back at you, he won't want to quit and make you look right.

If this beautiful child makes decisions that conflict

with other family members, the help is to release him without condemnation. Every experience is about unconditional love. His wisdom will always lead him to knowledge about himself, and all that comes along that path is helpful.

His decisions bring him the results of his thinking, just as yours do. When he chooses what conflicts with the rest of the family, there's no good reason for everyone else to suffer. Tell him the truth, that he isn't welcome as a disturbing factor, and when he's ready to contribute instead of take, he'll be welcome back. You may think this sounds cruel, especially if the child is young. Where can he go when he isn't old enough to take care of himself?

If he's old enough to try something, he's old enough to hear the consequences from doing so. Talk honestly, like you would with anyone disrupting your serenity. Tell him he's free to adopt whatever directions seems interesting, but if he chooses what's harmful to the rest of you, he'll have to find some other place to experiment.

This is what he'll face when he leaves you, isn't it? Show him what happens when he brings disruption to those he's with. This is the education he's looking for. There doesn't have to anger or ridicule in your sharing, only truth. Tell him you'd expect him to feel the same way if your behavior turned unloving. Children don't find it difficult to turn the situation around. They're open to what works.

Teach him as soon as you can what it means to be

the all powerful God he is. This means letting him see the results of his choices. Even though one night out in the cold may seem like a harsh ultimatum, it doesn't compare to a lifetime out there. And more than likely, he'll listen to how you plan to handle the situation and wait until he feels ready to face the consequences. When that time comes, he'll probably be dealing with different choices anyway, having moved into the realm of accountability for self.

All of this only works if you take responsibility for your decisions too; i.e., making sure he understands you mean what you say and intend to carry through with love and consideration for the rest of the family. When you act according to the strength of your own caring convictions, he gets a good look at powerful autonomy.

What else could there be to give your children? They come with the personality they need, the looks they want, the intelligence that's helpful, and the love of God in their hearts. All that their journey has to provide is wrapped up in understanding their own powerful energy and what it can generate.

This decade has its own particular challenges. In ten years, others will surface. In twenty, more. But whatever tool God uses to practice his autonomy, he is always searching for responsible action.

Whatever your child is using to challenge himself, your help is your wisdom, acceptance and love in whatever dosage he happens to need. It doesn't matter if you think his choices are wise. He has his own measure of priorities. If he didn't have tastes that differed from yours, you'd probably worry about his growth.

Other issues that come under the young adult's scrutiny fall into the current fad category. Pressure to have the right hairdo, clothes, music, and friends. Let go of your rigidity for superficial standards. If you bother your children about issues that are clearly their own business, they won't welcome your advice about knowing progress.

Why would they want to conform to your tastes in favor of theirs? Why are they wrong and you right? If you argue about the height of a skirt, or the length of a haircut, you put yourself in a position of weakness in your child's eyes. Making a transitory experiment like fashion the focus of your authority, forces him to question your wisdom in every area of discussion.

He's thinking in terms of a whole life spread out in front of him, with millions of wonderful options. Next week, a new direction may seem more appealing and he wants the freedom to switch delights without harassment.

Change places with him for a day. What if he were nagging you about every single preference you had; ridiculing your clothes for work every morning, making fun of your haircut in front of your friends, criticizing the music whenever you turned on the radio, challenging your extra-curricular activities as meaningless. How long would you put up with this abuse without some form of retaliation? Doesn't your child deserve the same consideration you expect?

When you give it to him, the results will astound you. But God isn't surprised when miracles occur. He knows why communication flourishes and it always has to do with allowing freedom to be, do, say, act and love in whatever way is enjoyable.

The only time you have to concern yourself with your child's peer pressures is when he asks for help in remaining autonomous. If he comes to you complaining about trouble staying comfortable in his own preferences, this is your opportunity to display your faith in his wisdom.

He doesn't want your high and mighty exhibition of acumen, he wants your reassurance of his own. Remind him he is the one who lives with the consequences of his actions, not his friends. He is the one who either feels good or bad about what happens, not his friends. He is the one who either suffers or delights from his choices, not his friends. He is the one who puts his life on the line, not his friends. He is the one who leaves your home from destructive behavior, not his friends. This is the advice that makes him sit up and take notice. This is the powerful seat of autonomy he's looking for. And this is the manner in which he will copy your behavior without the slightest hesitation or apology.

This philosophy is about taking responsibility for yourself wherever you are, whatever your age and whatever it's about. All that you're looking for is wrapped up in this thought.

You need to give him the real prize; the belief in himself. It's the only advice he'll always welcome because it's the only search he's really on.

**TEMPTATIONS
ARE HEALTHY AND INSTRUCTIVE
IF INVESTIGATED
FOR SPIRITUAL SATISFACTION.**

CHAPTER 19

Parenting / Career

**ONLY ONE CAREER IS EVER HAPPENING.
EVERYTHING ELSE
IS JUST THE MEANS FOR FINDING IT.**

***

Whether your career is homemaking, banking, teaching, music, carpentry, or any of the other millions of vocations, the only purpose it serves is to expand your understanding of love. Therefore, if you're trying to combine more than one, that's the path you believe has progress.

But only one career is really manifesting here on Earth, and everyone is sharing the same one. Your goal is to know yourself. When this happens, other careers just join the fun of the only one that matters. Until then, pursue the ones that light up your energy because that's how you find your ultimate success.

If you believe you are better served by combining child rearing with another major interest, the real issue becomes how to allot your time for everything you want. It could be anything taking opportunity away from parenting and the problem would remain.

It would appear this predicament of combining job and family is a female upheaval, because men have always been doing this. Perhaps some reevaluating is in order, and this generation wants to deal with it.

God doesn't look at the Earth and see male and female. He sees light beings looking for a happier way to live. Some of these auras feel they've been restricted in their choices and, so therefore, are trying to break away from stereotypes and limitations.

If the entities with this particular goal are men, God has the same tenderness and caring for their growth. He doesn't respond to gender, just to the cry for help. So in order to talk about this subject fairly, it's to reassure you that this issue is about the removal of confines, not about who gets to do what.

It isn't a matter of where the power lies, because for each, it lies wherever serenity is found. It isn't about who brings in the income or who tends the children, it's about each soul finding the comfort zone for living. Whether you're a male or female trying to do justice to both of these roles, the solution is the same.

There isn't any answer that's going to suddenly make time where it didn't exist before. You only have so much to divide between your interests. Where you give it in one area, you won't have it to give in another. But that doesn't mean the time you do have for each, can't be meaningful. You must become honest about where priorities sit comfortably, and then give your enthusiasm to whatever that is.

Parenting is whatever you make it, and so is your career. And so is your everything whatever you happen to be doing with your energy. Just because this chapter is about managing home and career with serenity, doesn't keep you from trying whatever you need, growing towards whatever goal you have.

The game that's being played is the same whether it's a woman or a man, and when your society looks at parenting and wage earning as joint endeavors where equal partnership is honored, the problem will disappear.

Stress only enters the situation when there's judgement that something is wrong when a man or a woman wants both. And as the society starts accepting this new direction as equitable and nourishing for all concerned, outer accoutrements will begin to support it accordingly.

Often, however, instead of loving the thrill of whatever choices are made, you worry if your decision is wrong. If I choose to stay at home, will I miss my chance for a successful career? If I go to work, will I miss my chance to be a good parent? If I try to do both, will I be cheating my children of their due, denying my mate of what is deserving, and running myself ragged in the bargain?

The children aren't going to suffer from anything except your denial of self-love. For a long time, men have gone to work and nurtured their offspring when accessible. Have children suffered because of this? Haven't they just expected him to do what he does? As long as they receive his tender devotion when he's around, they haven't cared in the slightest.

Why would they feel differently if their mother took this role unless someone conveys the message that she's doing something wrong? This is the disturber of peace and the robber of serenity; the doubt that the situation is just fine the way it is. And conversely, if the man wants to nurture from the home position, while the woman opts for the wage earner, isn't it just the wrong judgement that causes disharmony?

Combining family life and career, loves each person as much as the love they give to it. God doesn't say, with bilateral careers, you'll make it impossible for me to bring joy into your lives. He says, bring heaven to yourself by choosing the lifestyle that gives you serenity, and then have the courage to enjoy it.

When you select a busy life in terms of family and career, this is your decision. Don't treat your position disrespectfully as if you just got dumped into it unknowingly and are a victim of circumstances. Because if you do, you'll find yourself in circumstances that victimize you. Take the reins of your life, and wake up to your own resolutions.

If working and raising a family is necessary because you're the sole support, this is your determination too. Don't be fooled by what looks like chance. If you weren't eager to face this branching out, you wouldn't be experiencing it.

If you can't accept this theory, that life is running according to your own needs and desires, it won't change anything, will it? You still have to cope with whatever is happening. Every day comes with whatever challenges are present and you must deal with them regardless of your philosophy.

On the other hand, if you take the possibility that what you have is welcome and you wanted it for one reason or another, it does put you in a position of wisdom. It does put you in a position of someone who knows what he's doing. It does put you in the position of someone who's willing to look for what you thought was valuable.

If you have a choice about how to view life, isn't it more reassuring to consider that you do have some control? Isn't it more serene to believe that life isn't haphazard? Won't it help you appreciate what's with you as more valuable? Would you rather enjoy the process or hate it?

Your children are the same wise energy you are. They have agreed to participate in this particular drama with the same autonomy you have. Act like they have, and you'll find they respond more favorably to the exercise they're undertaking. Bring them into this challenge as co-creators and you'll find an interesting new attitude developing. Once you get rid of your own victim concept, your children will reconsider their role in this venture too.

God believes whatever your life manifests is what you believe is loving progress, and he's thrilled to support you in whatever that is. He doesn't think, what a hardship you've taken on. He thinks, here's an interesting choice to remember that loving coexistence is the only real event transpiring.

Give whatever you can to those you're with, tenderly caring for yourself first. How can your children grow up to respect themselves if they don't have a good example of what that means? When you face your daily routine wondering how you'll manage, look for the ways you've loved yourself from the path you've chosen.

If you're interested in trying out a new one and your mate is resistant, ask yourself why. Where is the loss in his imagination? Resistance comes when deprivation is believed in. If instead, benefits are anticipated, cooperation has a better chance to manifest.

Children aren't going to suffer unless they feel tension, mistrust, and blame around them. If they see two people learning to compromise and talk through disagreements, they gain a tolerance level for doing the same.

When the challenge becomes—which one has the right to decide the direction of another—ask why either of you should conform to the other's preconceived notions of progress. Remove your demands for that person to adapt to your interpretation of happiness if you want the demands on yourself to manifest serenity.

Each partner must feel he can accelerate his learning without permission from the other. If you block this from happening because of an insecurity about your own safety in the relationship, you're sabotaging the very idea you hope to promote.

You want to be important to your mate. You want to be respected for your contribution. You want to know that your opinion counts. You want to be free to pursue opportunities. You want to know that your usefulness is honored. Well, if you can't give this to another, you aren't going to find it for yourself. Nothing comes to you unless you're able to give it away because this is the opening in your aura to receive it. Therefore, whatever restrictions you exact from another, you put upon yourself. And as you refuse to open your heart to what another needs for progress, you close the door for progress to come to you.

The only comfortable role is to live in freedom. What this means is subjective, since each entity defines this term according to his own perception of love. But if you support your mate in whatever he deems as constructive releasing, while still honoring your own direction, harmony will reign.

If you bring this spirit of sustenance to your partner in parenting, your children will be learning about their path to emancipation. They only want to understand how to live in peaceful coexistence as they pursue their own vision of heaven.

Make the belief in their nurturing, the belief in your own. This is the formula for caring for those in your life. You can't be tending others successfully if you're forgetting to tenderly care for yourself. And caring for yourself means releasing others to the wisdom of their own integrity.

Have faith that if you live in a society where it's necessary for two incomes to sustain your family, you believe that this reality is productive to your soul's progress. Belief in your own autonomy can permeate every thought about your life. It puts you in the position of gratitude for your blessings as opposed to always thinking that life is unfair, difficult, unpredictable and fearful.

While you're here, you have things to learn, beauty to find, wisdom to embrace and people to love. All that you are living is giving it to you.

**MANY CAREERS ARE GOING
ON AS YOU RAISE YOUR CHILDREN,
AND NO ONE IS MORE OR LESS IMPORTANT
THAN ANOTHER.**

CHAPTER 20

Step-Parenting

THIS "STEP" HAS A
WONDERFUL CONNOTATION.
IT JUST MEANS THERE WAS A STEP
IN BETWEEN YOUR FINDING EACH OTHER.

***

Daring ideas have daring results because the energy it took to create them is excited about the results; i.e., the artist who can't wait to evidence his vision; the musician who runs to his instrument to find his dream inspired melody; the writer who finds a plot for his story; and the human who understands his reason for being. All of the sudden, the rest of the creation falls into place, the surrounding accompaniment starts to make sense, and the whole becomes workable as the focus becomes defined.

This is what step-parenting brings because all of a sudden, the participants are forced to deal with what life is all about; working together in harmony. The children have grown up with one set of rules and suddenly there's a new authority to deal with. The baby who knows what his cry will bring him, must experiment with new approaches to achieve his goal. Parents have to blend techniques to find a common ground that works for both. And all the while these testings proceed, sparks are flying as the whole tries to find comfort within itself.

Step-parenting is a microcosm of the world in it's struggle to love; the play whereby the actors need to ad-lib to make the scene work with the new cast of characters. It's the melting pot of emotions that come together to sift through the useless flailing to find the power of constructive cooperation. It's where God gets a chance to witness what works and what doesn't and why.

It's no accident that this metamorphosis is happening as humans take more interest in the worthiness of their lives. This emergence of self-love is reflecting the attitude that says, I deserve happiness, and nothing is written in stone that says I can't search for it any way I can discover. With this challenging and worthy goal in mind, light enters the worthy challenge that finds it's reward.

When major snags turn what could be blessed healing into painful sores, the balance of loving cooperation has been tipped. Someone is refusing to respect the other members of the experiment. Someone is believing there is only one way to live. Someone is balking at the many methods for expressing the love of God. One person's needs are overshadowing another's. And the miracle is always found from honoring the integrity of the whole.

How does one honor the integrity of the whole if one part of it refuses to cooperate? By keeping the well being of the unit as the focus of your decisions. When one member disrupts the peaceful coexistence of the whole, the whole needs to regroup in love. And this means to ask the agitator to either opt for love, or leave.

If you're in a situation where this concept isn't embraced, don't look for things to improve. When disrupters are given freedom to continue their behavior, the behavior expands. If you can't find the strength to make the well being of the whole your focus, don't be surprised when it falls apart.

Children are always testing. They can't help it. It's the most natural instinct there is. To the youngster, controlling adults is a heady power. If he can manipulate through this avenue, why would he give it up? Humanness is an experiment to understand strength in matter, and if tantrums, deception and threats get him this, why would he relinquish it?

If you let his behavior overrule your better judgement, you leave the workable unit in favor of tyranny. This arrangement will disband quickly, as the other members seek out a more comfortable working whole.

If you want this disturbing entity to rethink what creates power, you have to rethink the power you give him. Show him it doesn't work. How? By asking him to cooperate or test elsewhere.

Because every family unit goes through changes when the members either shrink or expand, each has to redefine his place in the whole when this happens. The reason step-parenting can be so fraught with power struggles is because no one understands what their new position will be. Even the parents have to negotiate their liability to the whole.

God's love manifests when all are able to consider the entire group. It's an auspicious beginning for those who can lovingly maneuver through this experiment. Cooperation is tested to its fullest.

All who work on this particular game are as closely related as the original family units. And their decision to be together is conceived in the same beauty that got the original clan together. And when these groupings form, those who have the biggest challenges with each other, have the closest ties in heaven.

What could be more beautiful than finding energy in matter that you adored before you came? And if your desire in entering this blessed fantasy on Earth was to remember that worthiness has nothing to do with choices, wouldn't it be challenging for your best friends to be in different ones? Wouldn't it be fun to eventually return to the "everything" of your heritage, and rejoice that nothing so transitory as humanness kept you from recognizing your beloveds?

Consider this possibility when you have difficulty dealing with step-children. Can you accept them in full acknowledgement for whoever they are, without making them wrong for the paths they've chosen?

Children arriving into your life through this route have the same Godly devotion to knowing you as anyone else. And your relationship with them is about the same release.

Although it may seem like a fluke of luck that brought you together, the passion God has for his progress doesn't allow for happenstance. The play is always unfolding in a caress that sweetly tends each participant. Growth is what you life is about; compassion for self and flexibility with new ideas is what makes your journey exciting. Step-children know how to test you in this direction, don't they? Be the twig that can bend in the wind instead of the one that gets snapped off because it stays so rigid.

Put yourself in the position where nothing destroys your ability to weather the storm. What enables this? It comes from placing your own best interests in the middle of whatever is happening. How can this possibly solve disharmony? How can it possibly not? When you're in discomfort, you just spread it around. When you're in serenity, others have a better chance of finding it.

How can you be the twig that bends and still honor your own needs? You do it by releasing others to find their own way of weathering the storm. This is how they find harmony.

Step-children only bring a bigger challenge than your own when you believe their previous lifestyle doesn't measure up to yours; i.e, something is wrong with how they were raised, something about them has to change if they're going to live with you, something about them is in need of improvement, or something about them isn't right.

You really don't need to learn anything new to be

a good step-parent, you just need to accept the new family as a part of yourself; the current reflection that speeds your journey into more of the whole you're searching for. If you look for how your compassion, understanding and tolerance have grown, you've found your reward.

HOW YOU FIND YOUR FELLOW GODS
IS AN EVER EXPANDING THOUGHT PROCESS,
AND ANY WAY THAT WORKS
WILL BE VALUED AS WORTHY.

Adoption

CAN YOU POSSIBLY GIVE YOURSELF
MORE THAN YOU HAVE?
YES,
IF YOU'RE WILLING TO ADOPT A NEW IDEA.

***

What is adoption? Once you answer this question, you have the answer to whatever you want to know about it. If the desire to adopt is embraced within your soul, the desire to be adopted is embraced within another. It is one means by which Godly light gets together for the purpose of finding unconditional love. Therefore, adoption is the caring way that some humans learn about themselves.

The only difference between this and any other form of child rearing is the route by which you find each other. And since God delights in his imaginative games, this is one he finds quite dazzling.

Suppose some wonderful soul starts off on his human journey with beautiful expectations for devotedly raising a family. As he wends his way through highs and lows, detours sometimes take him in unexpected directions. Nevertheless, he knows what he needs, who he wants to find, and why it's important. So even though he may lose his way here and there, never does he forgot his inner longings.

Spirit in transition who wants to join his journey stays alert to all nuances of his adventure, and whether or not his coupling produces offspring, these two souls will meet in whatever way they can create the opening. His heart knows what it wants, spirit in transition knows what it wants, so they make it happen through adoption, that's all.

Would God deny you your heart's desire? Would God say, sorry, you can't have what your human trip is for? Would God ever leave you without the means for learning what you came here to understand? How could he, when he is the love within you? Wherever your longings will reward you with light, God is answering your prayers.

This is a good time to talk about the difference between a "want" and a "need." God in matter may think he wants many different things for many different reasons, but the soul who directs the drama understands whether they're useful. If the "want" doesn't have progress, it isn't going to manifest. You, as the conscious awareness can either accept this beautiful truth, or continually believe you don't have what you should.

God can't be denied his reason for being here. He will find the souls he wants to, and he will do it in whatever way will love him. Conversely, what he doesn't find, he doesn't need.

This is where serenity is either found or remains illusive. The person who loves the blessings of his life, will find contentment. The person who can't, will be dissatisfied.

After all, if you can't appreciate the process of your life, what else is there? Each day comes and each day goes, and whether it's been worthwhile depends on the worthiness you've found in it.

If you want to conceive children, enjoy the process by which this happens. If you decide to adopt, find pleasure in this. For those who find themselves childless, look for the blessings in this eventuality. You must have hoped for it in this moment of time, or the God within would have brought something different.

Adoption is really just one way of finding the dear hearts who want to share your journey. When it comes to explaining your particular route to finding each other, use the principles founded in truth. This is what sets you all free into love. As you knowingly open your heart to whatever the child is curious about, you build a lasting bond of friendship that overshadows all disruptions that alter the caring love of God.

Children can sense when they're ready to hear about their emergence into matter, whatever route they've chosen. You only need to respond to their inquiries when they occur.

Don't be afraid to confess your longing to find this entity. He was feeling the same. Build on your shared insight that remembers the brilliant merging of love finding love, and express your joyous reception of his answer to your prayers.

Thank him for loving you enough to join your dream. Tell him how determined you were to find him, so he can relive the excitement he felt in responding. Treasure the joy these tender hearts bring into your life and never forget the adoring love they've given you.

REGARDLESS OF THE
CIRCUMSTANCES OF BIRTH,
ENERGY FINDS WHO IT'S LOOKING FOR.
SOMETIMES IT JUST HAS
A DIFFERENT CREATIVE APPROACH.

CHAPTER 22

Divorce

DIVORCE ASKS FOR RELEASE, NOT SEPARATION.
IF YOU FOCUS ON THE FIRST AND NOT THE SECOND,
GROWTH IS WAITING.

***

Jousting from rage to rage has no answers. It will only keep you in a state of limbo. If you're ever going to find answers that satisfy your heart, you must give up the idea of blame. No one is to blame for a divorce no matter how many reasons you think there are to make the other person wrong. Divorce comes when all, including the children, are ready to move on. Whether it's filled with agony or expectation is up to you.

Many undergoing this transition think the pain will lessen if they find as many faults with their antagonist as possible, while enlisting the support of friendships to confirm their convictions. This may have temporary relief, but the action/reaction of the universe is going to bring you exactly what you mete out, so don't be surprised when other blaming hearts join you.

When it comes to dealing with parenting while undergoing divorce, the only kindness to your children is to include them in whatever discussions take place. When they don't have a chance to join this interaction, they're left to their own devises for imagining what happened. And since they still believe the universe revolves around them, very often, they take all the responsibility onto themselves.

Unless they can gain some understanding of what went wrong, they won't have the tools to deal with it. Don't worry about how much information is appropriate. Depending on his maturity, the child will ask what he wants to know. You just need to respect his inquisitiveness and respond honestly.

If the parents don't take the blame as their excuse for divorce, the child won't be forced to take sides, and this frees him up to ask what's really on his mind.

You may think you're the one who deserves the child's loyalty because you see yourself as the wronged party. You aren't doing yourself a favor if you push for this response. Youngsters may temporarily make you right if you make them feel guilty enough. But children don't believe in loss, and if you are the reason they suffer this, they won't love you for it.

How will you enter into loving relationships after this one? Don't you hope for more caring and understanding? If you have carried your rightness to the extreme, the only aura that feels comfortable with yours is the one who sees the rightness of his ideas. Then, instead of moving into a more flexible relationship, you instead find more rigidity.

If this isn't what you hope to create, you must

rearrange your thought patterns about what happened last time. When you take responsibility for your contribution to whatever disruption manifested, your next relationship will reflect your belief in compromise and clemency.

Children give you the means for forgiving much easier, don't they? Most people don't want to hurt their children. They want them to grow up to be tolerant, compassionate, merciful human beings, filled with confidence to overcome hardships. This is your chance to show them how it's done.

Often, divorce can put you in the position of suddenly needing to reaffirm your self-respect even if you're the spouse who wants to leave. When you can accept the worthiness of the partner, regardless of what has transpired between the two of you, you find your own worthiness very quickly. This is the example that helps your children find theirs.

Why does it work this way? Because the open heart who can say—all are the energy of God trying to understand love—will find this understanding heart of God in all who surround him.

The kindest and most loving stance you can take for your children, is the very stance that God recommends for you; release, empathy, forgiveness, understanding, and blessings for the future.

Consider how your partner will feel when you release him to whatever adventure he longs for. And if you can't imagine this feeling, put yourself in the position of receivership. Wouldn't you be ecstatic for such sensitivity? And as you release your antagonist, he ceases to be one. Instead, he'll look to you with gratitude for your compassion of his journey.

As your children recognize you aren't going to put them in the middle of choosing sides, they also enjoy the relief that goes with the freedom to openly love whoever they care about.

Divorce isn't the end of devotion unless you bring hate to all that you felt. And divorce can be a time of wonderful growth if you allow it. Every possible scenario that manifests into separation could be discussed here, and never would one come up that couldn't be handled with kindness.

The reason it gets out of hand is because God forgets the action/reaction theory and all that it procreates. I'm sure you'd agree that no one ever intentionally brings greed, avarice, revenge, fear, hate or injustice into their lives. To the contrary, everyone is trying to avoid this and find serenity, love and joy. But you can't give one and receive another.

Your aura is filled with whatever thoughts you put there, and whatever they are, creates your universe. If you're counting on finding someone much more caring, gracious and tenderly devoted to you, you better make this what you give to others. The person who handles his life this way isn't going to find you, if you don't. He's going to find the person who goes through life the way he does.

Your children give you the best possible opportunity to learn this concept because you have so many good reasons to look out for their well being. Perhaps you've forgotten how much it meant to you to spend contented moments with your parents. How much did you want to respect them? Didn't you hope for an easy friendship?

Whether you actually found closeness or not, the desire was felt. Every child longs for it and the person who steps between them and this experience, is eventually going to suffer a damaged image. It might not happen for a while, but your children are going to lives full lives too. Sooner or later they'll reconsider such harshness towards a person searching for love, and you may not fare too well in the comparison.

Children instinctively want to forgive and move on without resentments. But they also want to keep your love. Let them have both and this is what they'll return to you.

They're learning what works as they watch you maneuver through the obstacles you create. Show them that everyone is deserving of honor and respect, regardless of what they need in order to be happy. This is what will bring you love and respect, regardless of what you need to find yours.

Parting with material things can sometimes be traumatic, especially for children. They've grown up with their surroundings a certain way. So very often with divorce, they not only go through the disruption of the cast of characters, but also a change of scenery. What was once beautifully familiar, becomes the unknown.

If the division of property is going to leave your little ones with less than they had before, this is your opportunity to assure them that material wealth can never be the origin of serenity. Make this transition as easy as you can for them, by finding the fun in whatever they do have. This teaches that "things" can come and go, but love is always present if the heart is willing to welcome whatever arrives.

Children worry that divorce will mean the loss of love. Their worst fears are realized if you deny them the presence of someone who cares for them. Whether it's the spouse, the grandparents, the cousins, or whoever, they need to feel the continuity of those whose love has caressed their path. Don't make them suffer for your angers. This is a time when they need the most affection they can find. Don't deny them the opportunity of finding it in the most obvious place; with those who cherish them the most.

Healing the pain from this challenge can be found and will be if you remember where to look for it. It won't come from holding on to the past. It won't come from haranguing the person who wants to leave. It won't come from forcing the children to take sides. It won't come from revenge. It won't come from criticizing. And it won't come from blame. It comes from finding the love in whatever happens. And this is the answer no matter what transition you're going through.

Remember the good times and look forward to the

wide open future ahead of you. Release your mate from reprisals and let him go forth with your well wishing. Speak well of him in front of the children, honoring him the same way you hope to be honored.

Instead of arguing for what is your due, trust that your new found friendship will be enough to illicit fair mindedness from the other. Take responsibility for what happened, looking for the benefits it will bring.

If you don't, then after the battle about getting divorced has subsided, the war about who gets what will go into gear. The more importance you put on the materiality you demand, the more your children will believe this is the source of happiness. How could they not? If you are in apoplexy about not receiving what you think you must have, then they're going to assume that without it, your life won't have meaning. Is this the message you want them to receive?

If you have tried your very best to solve things peacefully with respect and honor for everyone involved, you'll bring others into your life who treat you the same. And they will arrive regardless of whether your ex is around to help.

Ask what paralyzes you into such dread that you go to extremes to receive support from a reluctant participant. Isn't it the fear that if the help doesn't come from this one person, it won't arrive? Would God deny you what you deserve, simply because your ex doesn't want to give? Would God ever say, sorry, but there's only one source of abundance, and if you can't get it from there, that's it for you?

Stay focused on the goodness of whatever you had together. This is what turns everything around. You won't feel like a victim if you can value the gains. It may not seem that advantages are possible in the first embitterments, but they're always there.

Just as you suffer because you focus on pain, you need to focus on the positive to experience it. If you can find this possibility, you'll help your children do the same and everyone will move through this drama much easier.

God doesn't want his beautiful energy to suffer, he wants it to grow. This is always the challenge. Look for it in whatever you take on, and your children have a head start towards enjoying their own.

NO ONE IS EVER SEPARATED.
YOU ONLY FEEL LIKE IT
IF YOU STOP LOVING.

CHAPTER 23

Spiritual Training

**THE SPIRIT
IS THE ONLY THING YOU CAN'T TRAIN
WHILE HERE.
IT'S FREE FROM RESTRICTIONS
SO YOU CAN ONLY HONOR ITS SOVEREIGNTY.**

***

Ask what any training is supposed to do; teach how to function in that milieu, right? So to receive help in training the spirit, the parent first has to understand what the spirit is trying to accomplish. And unless you have the right goal in mind, the training isn't going to work.

How do you achieve happiness? This is the only education the spirit needs. And if you can figure it out for yourself, you won't have any difficulty helping your children.

Lamenting the sad state of the world's moral fiber isn't going to help your child find spiritual values. It will only teach him to blame others for what's lacking. Nothing happening "out there" has any effect on what's happening in the heart anyway, so spiritual training is done autonomously.

If you instruct your child in the virtues of ethically moral behavior, be sure you understand what this means. God is the source of everything worthwhile because he personifies the goodness in man, so when you teach your child how to live a Godly life, be sure you're encouraging him to find the beauty of himself.

He won't be living morally if he's finding something wrong with other religions, other people or other nations. God thinks his goodness is everywhere, and to believe otherwise is to leave your Godliness.

Religion can only teach the amount of love that each individual is open to receive. And how well that particular training works, depends on whether the ideas embodied in the precepts feel comfortable within the energy receiving it.

No one ever learned information about enriching the spirit if they felt sad, uncomfortable or guilty while participating. The soul becomes brighter from receiving the nourishment it craves, and anything that restricts its freedom isn't going to help.

Spirit is in humanness to enjoy itself, so make sure you're encouraging what this includes. It's the only spiritual training he's looking for. If you're involved in a particular theology, look for all the beauty its tenets offer your life. This is what will make your child interested in supporting it.

And when he shuns another, simply because their source of pleasure comes through a different faith, reassure him that love is love regardless of where it's learned.

Spirit is here to get rid of restrictions, not to find them. It wants to soar into the sky of love where all are equally revered and honored whether they come from the same indoctrination or not. Whatever you value as loving, your child is bound to take a good look at. After all, he joined the person he believed had some wonderful insight. But if he sees that you don't really embrace the beauty of your particular credo, don't be surprised if he looks elsewhere.

Children are seeking the same thing you are. Where is the love? If they begin resisting what you insist is beneficial, perhaps you aren't showing them why it is. "Talk" won't do it for them. They're more inclined to believe what they feel. Demonstrate the enormous love you find from the beliefs you hold dear, and they'll want to join in the fun.

There have been millions of faiths since humanness began, and no one is better than another. And you aren't going to miss anything simply because you're involved in one and don't try the others. There's only one thing going on in all of them. If you miss it where you are, you won't find it where you go.

The spirit wants to know itself. This training begins the moment the child is born and continues into the forever he'll exist. To know himself is to find the intrinsic goodness of his soul. If he can find it in others, he's well on his way to success. As the parent of this curious energy, how can you further his education?

Your child is watching you carefully. How happy are your ideas making you? After all, he has a vested interest in watching if your beliefs work. Does your faith gives encouragement and support to you? Does he see the devout ritual you go through nourishing your serenity? Do you welcome all who want to join your secular experience? Is he greeted into the religious community with the same enthusiasm all other members of the family receive? Is the leader a benevolent friend who regards all his parishioners as equal? Do the teachings encourage the spirit to laugh, sing and be joyous? This is how he'll reach conclusions about the value of your ethics. This is where he'll notice if you practice what you preach. This is how he'll determine if your path interests him.

Spiritual training isn't something you give your child. He gives it to himself. You can only show him what works for you. But if it isn't helpful, don't be surprised if he ignores your particular instruction.

No one ever accomplishes this for another, anyway. It's an impossible equation. Just as you can't find more of what you love until you first find what you care about, the atom can't explode until it's felt its own components. It's a path that can be shared with others, but not experienced by them. Each must look within to discover the nature of itself. So as you instruct your child about the moral ethical behavior that makes life run smoothly, ask him to believe in the goodness of himself.

AFTER SPIRIT ENTERS HUMANNESS,
THE ONLY TRAINING IT REALLY SEEKS
IS TO REMEMBER ITSELF.

CHAPTER 24

Independence

REALITY HAS BUT ONE NAME - INDEPENDENCE -
AND UNTIL YOU FIND IT IN HUMANNESS
YOU'LL PRACTICE UNTIL YOU DO.

***

Where would everyone be if independence weren't the only true reality? Certainly not living here in the middle of matter. How would you get here if you weren't self-governing? Who would put you here? How would they know where to put you, and how would they know when you were ready to leave?

Independence is the only existence there is. Isn't that really how you live? You move when you feel restless, eat when you're hungry, sleep when you're tired, talk when you have something to say, go where you feel like being, and think with ideas that please you. It's obvious. So why doesn't everyone act like the autonomous energy they are? Because you simply don't believe it. And that's why you're here right now—to remember.

You can be the impetus behind this reawakening for your children, and as you remind them you remind yourself. Deep inside every parent's heart is the hope that his offspring will grow into the shoes that fit the God he is. If there's a lapse in memory about this goal, it's only temporary. And when you hold onto your children with fierce determination instead of letting them leap for freedom, you'll delay your own attainment.

The child who doesn't rebel against restraint may seem well adjusted temporarily. But eventually he's going to rethink his comfort zone because energy must have freedom in order to grow and formulate. Therefore, the way to keep a strong and open relationship with your loved ones is to encourage self-expression and support each person's shout for freedom. Your own emancipation finds expression as you do.

In this book, the focus is on the liberation of your children into the strong, autonomous entities they know they're capable of being. But the same principles work whether you're encouraging a business, a country or a nation towards independence. All need the same ingredients to prosper.

The knowledge that makes for strength has just as little to do with bullying between nations as it does with bullying between humans. Strength is what happens when you allow each grouping to play out it's own drama as you carry on with your own. As your children learn this concept with you, they take it out into their lives. And as they give it with kindness to everyone they know, the idea grows. But giving it individually is what makes the larger ideas find it.

Independent thinking in small groupings is what will bring it to larger ones. And there isn't any other way that change comes. If you want the philosophy of independence to be world wide, those who live in it have to feel there's a chance to be independent of you.

How can you expect a country to understand fair mindedness unless they have been given a fair chance to survive alongside their neighbors? If you were constantly belittling the people who lived next door to you, taking what you wanted whenever you felt like it, bossing them around to suit your own purposes, and treating them as if they didn't belong in the human race, would you expect them to trust you? Would you expect them to welcome your advise?

All transforming comes through individual change, one by one, as each takes responsibility for what he believes in, how he conducts himself, and where he places his priorities. Failure to do so on a personal level creates the country that acts the same. How could it be otherwise? All your nation is can be summed up in the totality of those who live there.

What happens when a government feels one way and a population feels another? There is change. In a country where it's easy to transform, the arrival of new direction is painless. Where it isn't, struggle accompanies. This is the same process at work in your own personal transformation.

And unless you can grasp the parallel of these two concepts, your own progress gets stymied. Not because you aren't willing to grow, and not because you aren't thrilled to help your children do the same.

But because they're exactly the same thought. God doesn't see any separation between countries releasing each other and individuals nurturing independence. To him, they're one and the same.

Flexibility is your greatest asset, whether moving through growth in your life, or shaping the destiny of a nation. Give God a chance to show you what works. Open your mind to every possibility before you automatically call it unproductive. The help that comes your way for whatever you hope to learn, is everything that happens. So before you call your life impossible to understand, be a little braver about today and what it offers for insight. This is why you thought it was such a good idea to be here.

Parenting was created through purposeful thought as a nurturing environment from which the birthing energy could refocus on the value of itself. The only way God holds onto every idea he loves is through the memory of it. And how he keeps his memory strong is by knowing every emotion within his capability.

Reproduction offers a new opportunity to find what somehow illuded spirit before; the freedom of life, whatever that means to each autonomous light being. And the only path towards this brilliant discovery is responsibility for every moment that life is. How could it be otherwise? If you aren't this self-reliant being, there is no meaning to life. It would be a mishmash of undirected energy just moving around without purpose or reason, with no place to be and nothing to do. And if this sounds familiar, it's just because you've taken this opinion and believed the lie.

The loss of your own power and the feelings that accompanied it, is what caused the illusion called death to begin with. The body doesn't die unless you can't remember how to keep it in the blessed eternity of your birthright. Beauty isn't found from any other belief because anything less won't satisfy you.

You can try them all, and you can even invent some more along the way. But nothing will ever fulfill your child's heart or yours until you remember the essence of yourself. It's the only prize with eternity wrapped up in it and God is too determined to settle for less.

Train your child as soon as you can that he doesn't need you for all that he longs to accomplish. Let him discover how easily he can master whatever he conceives. Encourage his emancipation. He knows what's realistic and what isn't. Foster respect and honor for what he does well, so he takes his good feelings into whatever comes up next. Believe in his abilities so he can sense your delight in whatever talents he thought were instructive. What more could there be to give your child? If he appreciates his energy and finds pleasure in his existence, what more can he find?

If you wonder why you're alive and how you got here and where you're going, the answer is that you're God who is forever; the energy that takes itself wherever it pleases. And the next destination will be whatever gets you closer to remembering this.

Are you the catalyst to help your child discover his eternity? He hopes to become one with himself and he can only sense this from feeling autonomous. Make his life as powerful as your influence can.

There reaches a point where only he can create his homecoming. Until then you can believe in his potential and encourage his search. To do this, you must value his independence. Let him test his powers where it's safe and friendly so that when he goes out into the world he'll take all the confidence he's found from knowing you. This is your gift to him; trust in the appropriateness of all he's chosen and the belief in how he'll use it.

Stay steadfast for what makes your life comfortable, because this is the guidance that helps him choose wisely. Make time for what's meaningful so he can appreciate that time well spent brings rewards. Allow yourself freedom to experiment with ideas so he can watch how easy it is to change his mind. Look for the same playfulness in work you give to leisure so that he thinks every part of life is endearing. Honor this creation that calls itself "you," so his life is filled with the honor called God.

YOUR CHILD WILL BELIEVE
EVERYTHING YOU LIVE.
WHAT DO YOU WANT HIM TO REMEMBER?

From this moment forward,
there will never again
be endings for you,
only beginnings.
How can I make this promise
when I don't even know you?
Because I do.
I know you as well as I know myself.
This realization,
and all that it portends,
is what allowed
"Loveparent" to manifest.

INDEX

A

Abnormality at birth: 27
Action/Reaction,
  with toddlers: 44
  pre-school: 45
  with blame: 123
  with thoughts: 126
Adolescent,
  individuality of: 105
Advice,
  worth listening to: 90
Answers, how to find: 25
Approval, parental: 41
Arguing, mealtime: 38
Atoms: 60, 99, 133
Attitudes,
  about discipline: 69-70, 89
  about diversity: 72
  pessimistic: 62-63
  something wrong: 67
  under scrutiny: 76
Aura,
  access to: 58
  reading it: 14-15, 27, 60
  misalignment of: 60
Autonomy: 101, 135

B

Beacon of light: 92
Behavior,

anger producing: 90
  appropriateness of: 56
Beliefs, the infant's: 55
Blame in divorce: 123
Birth,
  anticipation of: 3
  feelings at: 16, 23-24, 28
Bribery, habit of: 79

C

Career,
  male/female: 108
  reason for: 109
Change,
  struggling with: 137
Changing your mind: 139
Cherishing: 126
Choices,
  for diet: 36
  finding loved ones: 119
  fun of: 4
  having children: 3-4,
  regarding careers: 108
  why: 102, 115, 133
  understanding them: 95
Choosing sides,
  in divorce: 125
Co-creating: 111

why it fails: 115
how it succeeds: 115
unity: 117
Fear,
re receivership, 129
Flexibility: 137
Forever: 6
Forgetfulness,
of devotion: 24-25
Forgiveness,
need to: 127
phrase: 72
incentive for: 124-125
Formulating opinions: 31
Freedom
of expression: 17
of thought: 31
to choose diet: 37
to expand: 34
Friendship,
what kind you want: 47
what makes one: 32

G

Gadget phrase: 57
Gardens for growth: 91
Garden of Eden: 55
God,
his love for you: 24
his hopes for you: 25
his opinions: 111

his promises: 16
who he is: 138
Guilt,
relative to comfort: 131

H

Happiness,
for the spirit: 130
where it is: 132
Harmony, what it is: 23
Hatred, overcoming: 72
Health,
choices for: 27
promoting: 26
Healing, after divorce: 128
Hunger: 36

I

Independence,
as an earner: 81
asserting it: 96
of thought: 31
strength for: 91
with homework: 87
Individuality,
encouraging: 32
discouraging: 42
of dress: 94
respecting: 71
Infant,
bodily functions of: 54

Postal Orders:
Ascension Publishing, Betsy Thompson
P.O. Box 3001-890, Burbank, CA 91508 USA

Price:
$8.95, plus tax and shipping (see below)

Please send me a copy of LOVEPARENT. I understand that I may return the book for a full refund, for any reason, no questions asked.

COMPANY NAME_____

NAME_____

ADDRESS_____

CITY_____

STATE_____ZIP_____

Sales Tax:
Please add California 6.25% (56¢ per book)
for orders shipped to California addresses
(6.75%, or 60¢ per book in Los Angeles County).

Shipping:
Book Rate: $1.75 for the first book and 75 cents
for each additional book (surface shipments
may take three to four weeks).
Air Mail: Add $3 per book.